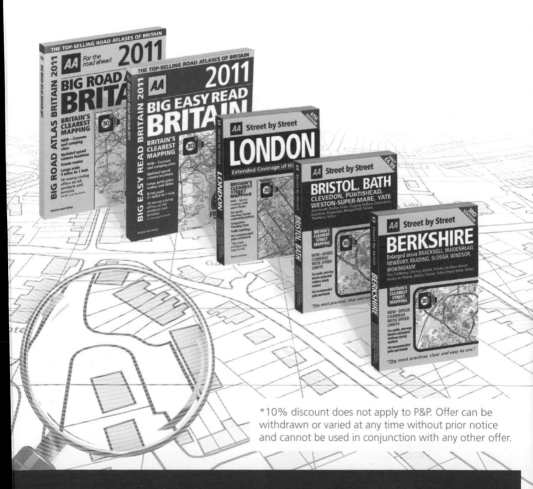

Get 10% off marked prices*
On AA Car Essentials

Keeping you prepared on the road

Simply visit **theAA.com/shop** and enter the promo code **DRIVERS2** at the checkout to claim your discount, terms and conditions apply.

AA For the road ahead

Theory Test for Car Drivers

The **official** questions and **answers** for **learner drivers**

Produced by AA Publishing.
© AA Media Limited 1996
First edition 1996, reprinted 1996 (5 times)
Second edition with revised questions 1997, reprinted 1998 (twice)
Third edition with revised questions 1998, reprinted with amendments 1998 (twice)
Fourth edition with revised questions 1999, reprinted 2000
Fifth edition with revised questions 2000
Sixth edition with revised questions 2001, reprinted 2002 (twice) and June 2002 with amendments
Seventh edition with revised questions 2003. Reprinted as a special edition June 2003. Reprinted 2003 and 2004.
Reprinted with amendments 2005
Eighth edition with revised questions 2006
Ninth edition with revised questions 2007, reprinted 2007
Tenth edition with revised questions 2008, reprinted 2008 with amendments, reprinted 2009 (four times)
Eleventh edition with revised introduction and case study examples 2010, reprinted January 2011

ISBN: 978-0-7495-6718-7

Published by AA Publishing (a trading name of AA Media Limited, whose registered office
is Fanum House, Basing View, Basingstoke, Hampshire RG21 4EA; registered number
06112600).

Visit AA Publishing at theAA.com/shop

Colour separation by Keene Group, Andover
Printed by Leo Paper Products, China

Image credits
Front and back cover: © National Motoring Museum/Alamy

A04636

Contents

About the Theory Test

You have to pass two driving tests before you can apply for a full driving licence. This book contains the official car questions from the Driving Standards Agency (DSA) that you may have to answer. You will have to pass both the question part and the hazard perception part to pass your Theory Test, before you can apply for the Practical Test.

The Theory Test consists of 50 questions, and a separate video clips section, called hazard perception. You will have 57 minutes to complete the question part of the test, using a touch-screen, and all questions are multiple-choice. You have to score 43 out of 50 on the theory questions to pass. The Government may, from time to time, introduce new or amended questions.

How to use this book

This book contains all the official questions for car drivers which appear in the question bank of the Driving Standards Agency (DSA). You could be tested on any of these questions when you take your touch-screen Theory Test.

The questions in this book are arranged in themes, such as Safety Margins and Hazard Awareness. Each theme has its own colour band, to help you find your way around. However, it is not cut and dried, and as you start to work through the questions you will soon discover that similar questions on the same topic may appear in different theme sections. Don't be put off by this, but read each question and the choice of answers very carefully. A similar question may be being asked in a different way, in order to test your full understanding.

You'll find all the correct answers to the questions at the back of the book. That way,

you can easily test yourself to see what you are getting right, and what you need to work on.

> Questions marked **NI** are **not** found in Theory Tests in Northern Ireland

How to study for the Theory Test
Remember
- Do not try too many questions at once.
- Do not try to learn the answers by heart.
- The order of the questions in this book may be different from how they are arranged in the actual test – so do not try to memorise the order.

How to answer the questions
Each question has four, five or six answers. You must mark the boxes with the correct answer or answers. Each question tells you how many answers to mark. Don't worry about accidentally missing marking an answer because you'll be reminded that you haven't ticked enough boxes before moving on to the next question.

Study each question carefully, making sure you understand what it is asking you. Look carefully at any diagram, drawing or photograph. Before you look at the answers given, decide what you think the right answer may be. You can then select the answer that matches the one you had decided on. If you follow this system, you will avoid being confused by questions that appear similar.

You can also answer the questions in any order you choose by moving forwards and backwards through the questions. You can also change your answer/s if necessary and flag questions you're unsure about, then go back to them later in the test. Your remaining time is shown on the screen throughout the test.

Case study questions

Case study questions were introduced to the Theory Test in September 2009, and are designed to test that you understand how to apply your knowledge of driving theory in a given driving situation.

Typically, five of the 50 questions in the Theory Test will take the form of a case study. All five questions will be based on a single driving situation and will appear one at a time during the multiple-choice part of your Theory Test. The questions are taken from the DSA's databank of Theory Test Questions (see pages 12–156) and have multiple-choice answers.

The case study questions in your Theory Test could be based on any driving situation and taken from a range of topics covered by the Theory Test syllabus. The following example has been put together by the AA to demonstrate how the case study will work in the 'real exam', so you'll know what to expect. This example will not appear in the Theory Test.

CASE STUDY 1

You need to go to the airport to pick up a relative that has been on holiday. The journey will take you on various roads including both A-roads and motorways.

As you start your journey it begins to rain and continues to get heavier as you drive.

You have not driven to the airport before but you have planned your route before leaving and feel confident about the journey.

1. You are following a vehicle on a wet road. You should leave a time gap of at least

Mark one answer

- [ ] one second
- [ ] two seconds
- [ ] three seconds
- [ ] four seconds

CASE STUDY 1

You need to go to the airport to pick up a relative that has been on holiday. The journey will take you on various roads including both A-roads and motorways.

As you start your journey it begins to rain and continues to get heavier as you drive.

You have not driven to the airport before but you have planned your route before leaving and feel confident about the journey.

2. What does this sign mean?

Mark one answer

- [ ] you have priority
- [ ] no motor vehicles
- [ ] two-way traffic
- [ ] no overtaking

Next

Back   Flag   Review   Next

CASE STUDY 1

You need to go to the airport to pick up a relative that has been on holiday. The journey will take you on various roads including both A-roads and motorways.

As you start your journey it begins to rain and continues to get heavier as you drive.

You have not driven to the airport before but you have planned your route before leaving and feel confident about the journey.

3. You have just gone through deep water. To dry off the brakes you should

Mark one answer

☐ accelerate and keep to a high speed for a short time

☐ go slowly while gently applying the brakes

☐ avoid using the brakes at all for a few miles

☐ stop for at least an hour to allow them time to dry

Back

CASE STUDY 1

You need to go to the airport to pick up a relative that has been on holiday. The journey will take you on various roads including both A-roads and motorways.

As you start your journey it begins to rain and continues to get heavier as you drive.

You have not driven to the airport before but you have planned your route before leaving and feel confident about the journey.

4. A bus has stopped at a bus stop ahead of you. Its right-hand indicator is flashing. You should

Mark one answer

☐ flash your headlights and slow down

☐ slow down and give way if it is safe to do so

☐ sound your horn and keep going

☐ slow down and then sound your horn

Next

CASE STUDY 1

You need to go to the airport to pick up a relative that has been on holiday. The journey will take you on various roads including both A-roads and motorways.

As you start your journey it begins to rain and continues to get heavier as you drive.

You have not driven to the airport before but you have planned your route before leaving and feel confident about the journey.

5. Where you see street lights but no speed limit signs the limit is usually

Mark one answer

☐ 30mph

☐ 40mph

☐ 50mph

☐ 60mph

Back   Flag   Review   Next

Answers to sample case study questions: 1D 2D 3B 4B 5A

Hazard perception

The video clips element of the Theory Test is known as hazard perception. Its aim is to find out how good you are at noticing hazards developing on the road ahead. The test will also show how much you know about the risks of driving, that is, risks to you as a driver, risks to your passengers and risks to other road users.

The test lasts for about 20 minutes. First you will be given some instructions explaining how it works; you will also get a chance to practise with the computer and mouse before you start the test 'for real'. This is to make sure you know what to expect on the test, and that you are happy with what you have to do.

Next you will see film or video clips of real street scenes with traffic such as motor vehicles, pedestrians, cyclists, etc. The scenes are shot from the point of view of a driver in a car. You have to notice hazards that are developing on the road ahead – that is, problems that could lead to an accident. As soon as you notice a hazard developing, click on the mouse control. You will have plenty of time to see the hazard, but the sooner you notice it, the more marks you will score.

Every clip has at least one hazard in it – some clips may have more than one hazard. You currently have to score 44 out of 75 to pass **but** the pass mark may change and it is advisable to check with your driving instructor or the Driving Standards Agency before sitting your test. (Note that the computer has checks built in to show up anyone trying to cheat – for example, someone who keeps clicking the mouse all the time!)

For each hazard you spot you get one or more points. The more quickly you spot the hazard developing on-screen, and click on it with the mouse, the higher your score. But be aware that each test clip will only be shown once. You will not have an opportunity to go back to an earlier clip and change your response, so you need to concentrate.

Remember, you have to pass both the theory questions and hazard perception to pass the Theory Test. At the end of the test they will tell you your scores for both parts. Even if you only failed on one part of the Theory Test, you still have to take both parts again next time.

Preparing for hazard perception

Learner drivers need more training in how to spot hazards, because they are often so busy thinking about using the car's controls that they forget to watch the road and traffic. Learner drivers and new drivers are up to two seconds slower at spotting hazards than more experienced drivers. Proper training can really help you to see more of the hazards that you will meet when driving, and to see those hazards earlier, so you're less likely to have an accident.

A hazard is anything that might cause you to change speed or direction when driving. The hazard perception element of the Theory Test is about spotting developing hazards. This is one of the key skills of good driving, and is also called anticipation. Anticipating hazards, such as car doors opening or children running into the road, means looking out for them in advance and taking the appropriate action.

As you get more driving experience you will start to learn about times and places where you are most likely to meet hazards. An example of this is the rush hour. You know that people take more risks when driving in the rush hour. Maybe they have to drop their children off at school before going to work. Maybe they are late for a business meeting or are in a hurry to get home. So you have to be prepared for bad driving, for example, other drivers pulling out in front of you.

Much of *The Highway Code* is about the hazards you find at junctions. You might be on a minor road and have to turn out on to a major road where you can't see clearly both ways; or you might be at a crossroads where there are no signs saying which vehicle has priority (should go first).

Your driving instructor has been trained to help you learn hazard perception skills, and can give you plenty of practice in what to look out for when driving, how to anticipate hazards, and what action to take when you have to deal with hazards of all kinds. You won't be able to practise with the real video clips used in the test, of course, but training books and practice videos are available.

Preparing for both tests

You are strongly recommended to prepare for the Theory Test at the same time as you develop your skills behind the wheel for the Practical Test. Obviously, there are many similarities between the two tests – it is all about helping to make you a safer driver on today's busy roads. By preparing for both tests at the same time, you will reinforce your knowledge and understanding of all aspects of driving and you will improve your chances of passing both tests first time.

Selecting a driving school

When you select a driving school to teach you the practical skills, make sure they are prepared to advise and help you with the Theory Test. Good driving schools will provide theory practice papers for you to complete before you take the real test. These papers will help you judge your level of knowledge and help with your preparation. Check with friends who have been taught recently, and make sure you understand the difference between an instructor who displays a pink badge or licence (a trainee instructor) and one who displays a green badge or licence (a fully qualified instructor).

Price is important, so find out whether the school offers any discounts for blocks or courses of lessons paid in advance; if you decide to pay in advance, make sure the driving school is reputable. If lesson prices are very low, ask yourself 'why?' Check how long the lesson will last, as some driving schools offer lessons of less than 60 minutes. And don't forget to ask about the car you'll be learning to drive in. Is it modern and reliable? Is it insured? Does it have dual controls? As with all courses, there are a number of subjects you will need to master. All good driving schools will have available a progress sheet and syllabus, which sets out all the skills you will need and keeps a record of your progress. You will probably find that if you take a two-hour lesson every week, your rate of progress will surprise you!

It is important that you should not take your Theory Test too early in your course of practical lessons. This is because you need the experience of meeting real hazards while you are learning to drive, so that you will be able to pass the hazard perception part of the Theory Test. You must pass the Theory Test

before you can take the Practical Test. Agree a plan of action with your driving instructor. After a few hours of driving tuition the instructor will discuss with you a structured course to suit your needs and you can agree on the likely date when you will be ready to take the Practical Test. Once you have passed your Theory Test, you can apply for a Practical Test appointment; this will give you added incentive to prepare thoroughly.

AA Driving School

The AA has a driving school that only uses fully qualified instructors, who are all familiar with the Theory Test, including case studies and hazard perception, and the Practical Test. Why not give them a try? You can ring for details on freephone 0800 60 70 80 or visit the website at **AAdrivingschool.co.uk**

Being a good driver is more than just having the knowledge and the skills – it is about applying them with the right attitude. No one is a 'natural' or a 'perfect' driver. All drivers make mistakes. Being careful, courteous and considerate to other road users will complement the skills and knowledge you will acquire in the coming weeks and make you a good and safe driver.

Further information

For more practical information on learning to drive including the Theory Test multiple-choice questions and hazard perception and the Practical Test visit **theAA.com** and **www.direct.gov.uk/motoring.** For information on the Pass Plus scheme visit **www.passplus.org.uk**

1 Before you make a U-turn in the road, you should

Mark one answer

- [ ] A. give an arm signal as well as using your indicators
- [ ] B. signal so that other drivers can slow down for you
- [ ] C. look over your shoulder for a final check
- [ ] D. select a higher gear than normal

2 As you approach this bridge you should

Mark three answers

- [ ] A. move into the middle of the road to get a better view
- [ ] B. slow down
- [ ] C. get over the bridge as quickly as possible
- [ ] D. consider using your horn
- [ ] E. find another route
- [ ] F. beware of pedestrians

3 When following a large vehicle you should keep well back because this

Mark one answer

- [ ] A. allows you to corner more quickly
- [ ] B. helps the large vehicle to stop more easily
- [ ] C. allows the driver to see you in the mirrors
- [ ] D. helps you to keep out of the wind

4 In which of these situations should you avoid overtaking?

Mark one answer

- [ ] A. Just after a bend
- [ ] B. In a one-way street
- [ ] C. On a 30mph road
- [ ] D. Approaching a dip in the road

5 This road marking warns

Mark one answer

- [ ] A. drivers to use the hard shoulder
- [ ] B. overtaking drivers there is a bend to the left
- [ ] C. overtaking drivers to move back to the left
- [ ] D. drivers that it is safe to overtake

6 Your mobile phone rings while you are travelling. You should

Mark one answer

- [ ] A. stop immediately
- [ ] B. answer it immediately
- [ ] C. pull up in a suitable place
- [ ] D. pull up at the nearest kerb

7 Why are these yellow lines painted across the road?

Mark one answer

- [ ] A. To help you choose the correct lane
- [ ] B. To help you keep the correct separation distance
- [ ] C. To make you aware of your speed
- [ ] D. To tell you the distance to the roundabout

8 You are approaching traffic lights that have been on green for some time. You should

Mark one answer

- [ ] A. accelerate hard
- [ ] B. maintain your speed
- [ ] C. be ready to stop
- [ ] D. brake hard

9 Which of the following should you do before stopping?

Mark one answer

- [ ] A. Sound the horn
- [ ] B. Use the mirrors
- [ ] C. Select a higher gear
- [ ] D. Flash your headlights

10 What does the term 'blind spot' mean for a driver?

Mark one answer

- [ ] A. An area covered by your right-hand mirror
- [ ] B. An area not covered by your headlights
- [ ] C. An area covered by your left-hand mirror
- [ ] D. An area not covered by your mirrors

11 Objects hanging from your interior mirror may

Mark two answers

- [ ] A. restrict your view
- [ ] B. improve your driving
- [ ] C. distract your attention
- [ ] D. help your concentration

12 Which of the following may cause loss of concentration on a long journey?

Mark four answers

- [ ] A. Loud music
- [ ] B. Arguing with a passenger
- [ ] C. Using a mobile phone
- [ ] D. Putting in a cassette tape
- [ ] E. Stopping regularly to rest
- [ ] F. Pulling up to tune the radio

13 On a long motorway journey boredom can cause you to feel sleepy. You should

Mark two answers

- [ ] A. leave the motorway and find a safe place to stop
- [ ] B. keep looking around at the surrounding landscape
- [ ] C. drive faster to complete your journey sooner
- [ ] D. ensure a supply of fresh air into your vehicle
- [ ] E. stop on the hard shoulder for a rest

14 You are driving at dusk. You should switch your lights on

Mark two answers

- [ ] **A.** even when street lights are not lit
- [ ] **B.** so others can see you
- [ ] **C.** only when others have done so
- [ ] **D.** only when street lights are lit

15 You are most likely to lose concentration when driving if you

Mark two answers

- [ ] **A.** use a mobile phone
- [ ] **B.** listen to very loud music
- [ ] **C.** switch on the heated rear window
- [ ] **D.** look at the door mirrors

16 Which FOUR are most likely to cause you to lose concentration while you are driving?

Mark four answers

- [ ] **A.** Using a mobile phone
- [ ] **B.** Talking into a microphone
- [ ] **C.** Tuning your car radio
- [ ] **D.** Looking at a map
- [ ] **E.** Checking the mirrors
- [ ] **F.** Using the demisters

17 Your vehicle is fitted with a hands-free phone system. Using this equipment whilst driving

Mark one answer

- [ ] **A.** is quite safe as long as you slow down
- [ ] **B.** could distract your attention from the road
- [ ] **C.** is recommended by *The Highway Code*
- [ ] **D.** could be very good for road safety

18 Using a hands-free phone is likely to

Mark one answer

- [ ] **A.** improve your safety
- [ ] **B.** increase your concentration
- [ ] **C.** reduce your view
- [ ] **D.** divert your attention

19 You should ONLY use a mobile phone when

Mark one answer

- [ ] **A.** receiving a call
- [ ] **B.** suitably parked
- [ ] **C.** driving at less than 30mph
- [ ] **D.** driving an automatic vehicle

20 You must not use a hand-held phone while you are driving. Using a hands-free system

Mark one answer

- [ ] **A.** is acceptable in a vehicle with power steering
- [ ] **B.** will significantly reduce your field of vision
- [ ] **C.** will affect your vehicle's electronic systems
- [ ] **D** could distract your attention from the road

21 What is the safest way to use a mobile phone in your vehicle?

Mark one answer

- A. Use hands-free equipment
- B. Find a suitable place to stop
- C. Drive slowly on a quiet road
- D. Direct your call through the operator

22 You are driving on a wet road. You have to stop your vehicle in an emergency. You should

Mark one answer

- A. apply the handbrake and footbrake together
- B. keep both hands on the wheel
- C. select reverse gear
- D. give an arm signal

23 When you are moving off from behind a parked car you should

Mark three answers

- A. look round before you move off
- B. use all the mirrors on the vehicle
- C. look round after moving off
- D. use the exterior mirrors only
- E. give a signal if necessary
- F. give a signal after moving off

24 You are travelling along this narrow country road. When passing the cyclist you should go

Mark one answer

- A. slowly, sounding the horn as you pass
- B. quickly, leaving plenty of room
- C. slowly, leaving plenty of room
- D. quickly, sounding the horn as you pass

25 Your vehicle is fitted with a hand-held telephone. To use the telephone you should

Mark one answer

- A. reduce your speed
- B. find a safe place to stop
- C. steer the vehicle with one hand
- D. be particularly careful at junctions

26 To answer a call on your mobile phone while travelling you should

Mark one answer

- A. reduce your speed wherever you are
- B. stop in a proper and convenient place
- C. keep the call time to a minimum
- D. slow down and allow others to overtake

27 Your mobile phone rings while you are on the motorway. Before answering you should

Mark one answer

- [ ] **A.** reduce your speed to 30mph
- [ ] **B.** pull up on the hard shoulder
- [ ] **C.** move into the left-hand lane
- [ ] **D.** stop in a safe place

28 You are turning right onto a dual carriageway. What should you do before emerging?

Mark one answer

- [ ] **A.** Stop, apply the handbrake and then select a low gear
- [ ] **B.** Position your vehicle well to the left of the side road
- [ ] **C.** Check that the central reservation is wide enough for your vehicle
- [ ] **D.** Make sure that you leave enough room for a vehicle behind

29 You lose your way on a busy road. What is the best action to take?

Mark one answer

- [ ] **A.** Stop at traffic lights and ask pedestrians
- [ ] **B.** Shout to other drivers to ask them the way
- [ ] **C.** Turn into a side road, stop and check a map
- [ ] **D.** Check a map, and keep going with the traffic flow

30 You are waiting to emerge from a junction. The windscreen pillar is restricting your view. What should you be particularly aware of?

Mark one answer

- [ ] **A.** Lorries
- [ ] **B.** Buses
- [ ] **C.** Motorcyclists
- [ ] **D.** Coaches

31 When emerging from junctions which is most likely to obstruct your view?

Mark one answer

- [ ] **A.** Windscreen pillars
- [ ] **B.** Steering wheel
- [ ] **C.** Interior mirror
- [ ] **D.** Windscreen wipers

32 Windscreen pillars can obstruct your view. You should take particular care when

Mark one answer

- [ ] **A.** driving on a motorway
- [ ] **B.** driving on a dual carriageway
- [ ] **C.** approaching a one-way street
- [ ] **D.** approaching bends and junctions

33 You cannot see clearly behind when reversing. What should you do?

Mark one answer

- [ ] **A.** Open your window to look behind
- [ ] **B.** Open the door and look behind
- [ ] **C.** Look in the nearside mirror
- [ ] **D.** Ask someone to guide you

34 When you see a hazard ahead you should use the mirrors. Why is this?

Mark one answer

- [ ] **A.** Because you will need to accelerate out of danger
- [ ] **B.** To assess how your actions will affect following traffic
- [ ] **C.** Because you will need to brake sharply to a stop
- [ ] **D.** To check what is happening on the road ahead

35 You are waiting to turn right at the end of a road. Your view is obstructed by parked vehicles. What should you do?

Mark one answer

- [ ] **A.** Stop and then move forward slowly and carefully for a proper view
- [ ] **B.** Move quickly to where you can see so you only block traffic from one direction
- [ ] **C.** Wait for a pedestrian to let you know when it is safe for you to emerge
- [ ] **D.** Turn your vehicle around immediately and find another junction to use

36 Your vehicle is fitted with a navigation system. How should you avoid letting this distract you while driving?

Mark one answer

- [ ] **A.** Keep going and input your destination into the system
- [ ] **B.** Keep going as the system will adjust to your route
- [ ] **C.** Stop immediately to view and use the system
- [ ] **D.** Stop in a safe place before using the system

37 You are driving on a motorway and want to use your mobile phone. What should you do?

Mark one answer

- [ ] **A.** Try to find a safe place on the hard shoulder
- [ ] **B.** Leave the motorway and stop in a safe place
- [ ] **C.** Use the next exit and pull up on the slip road
- [ ] **D.** Move to the left lane and reduce your speed

38 At a pelican crossing the flashing amber light means you MUST

Mark one answer

- A. stop and wait for the green light
- B. stop and wait for the red light
- C. give way to pedestrians waiting to cross
- D. give way to pedestrians already on the crossing

39 You should never wave people across at pedestrian crossings because

Mark one answer

- A. there may be another vehicle coming
- B. they may not be looking
- C. it is safer for you to carry on
- D. they may not be ready to cross

40 At a puffin crossing, which colour follows the green signal?

Mark one answer

- A. Steady red
- B. Flashing amber
- C. Steady amber
- D. Flashing green

41 The conditions are good and dry. You could use the 'two-second rule'

Mark one answer

- A. before restarting the engine after it has stalled
- B. to keep a safe gap from the vehicle in front
- C. before using the 'Mirror-Signal-Manoeuvre' routine
- D. when emerging on wet roads

42 'Tailgating' means

Mark one answer

- A. using the rear door of a hatchback car
- B. reversing into a parking space
- C. following another vehicle too closely
- D. driving with rear fog lights on

43 Following this vehicle too closely is unwise because

Mark one answer

- A. your brakes will overheat
- B. your view ahead is increased
- C. your engine will overheat
- D. your view ahead is reduced

44 You are following a vehicle on a wet road. You should leave a time gap of at least

Mark one answer

- A. one second
- B. two seconds
- C. three seconds
- D. four seconds

45 You are in a line of traffic. The driver behind you is following very closely. What action should you take?

Mark one answer

- A. Ignore the following driver and continue to travel within the speed limit
- B. Slow down, gradually increasing the gap between you and the vehicle in front
- C. Signal left and wave the following driver past
- D. Move over to a position just left of the centre line of the road

46 A long, heavily laden lorry is taking a long time to overtake you. What should you do?

Mark one answer
- [ ] **A.** Speed up
- [ ] **B.** Slow down
- [ ] **C.** Hold your speed
- [ ] **D.** Change direction

47 Which of the following vehicles will use blue flashing beacons?

Mark three answers
- [ ] **A.** Motorway maintenance
- [ ] **B.** Bomb disposal
- [ ] **C.** Blood transfusion
- [ ] **D.** Police patrol
- [ ] **E.** Breakdown recovery

48 Which THREE of these emergency services might have blue flashing beacons?

Mark three answers
- [ ] **A.** Coastguard
- [ ] **B.** Bomb disposal
- [ ] **C.** Gritting lorries
- [ ] **D.** Animal ambulances
- [ ] **E.** Mountain rescue
- [ ] **F.** Doctors' cars

49 When being followed by an ambulance showing a flashing blue beacon you should

Mark one answer
- [ ] **A.** pull over as soon as safely possible to let it pass
- [ ] **B.** accelerate hard to get away from it
- [ ] **C.** maintain your speed and course
- [ ] **D.** brake harshly and immediately stop in the road

50 What type of emergency vehicle is fitted with a green flashing beacon?

Mark one answer
- [ ] **A.** Fire engine
- [ ] **B.** Road gritter
- [ ] **C.** Ambulance
- [ ] **D.** Doctor's car

51 A flashing green beacon on a vehicle means

Mark one answer
- [ ] **A.** police on non-urgent duties
- [ ] **B.** doctor on an emergency call
- [ ] **C.** road safety patrol operating
- [ ] **D.** gritting in progress

52 A vehicle has a flashing green beacon. What does this mean?

Mark one answer
- [ ] **A.** A doctor is answering an emergency call
- [ ] **B.** The vehicle is slow moving
- [ ] **C.** It is a motorway police patrol vehicle
- [ ] **D.** The vehicle is carrying hazardous chemicals

53 Diamond-shaped signs give instructions to

Mark one answer
- [ ] **A.** tram drivers
- [ ] **B.** bus drivers
- [ ] **C.** lorry drivers
- [ ] **D.** taxi drivers

54 On a road where trams operate, which of these vehicles will be most at risk from the tram rails?

Mark one answer
- [ ] **A.** Cars
- [ ] **B.** Cycles
- [ ] **C.** Buses
- [ ] **D.** Lorries

55 What should you use your horn for?

Mark one answer

- A. To alert others to your presence
- B. To allow you right of way
- C. To greet other road users
- D. To signal your annoyance

56 You are in a one-way street and want to turn right. You should position yourself

Mark one answer

- A. in the right-hand lane
- B. in the left-hand lane
- C. in either lane, depending on the traffic
- D. just left of the centre line

57 You wish to turn right ahead. Why should you take up the correct position in good time?

Mark one answer

- A. To allow other drivers to pull out in front of you
- B. To give a better view into the road that you're joining
- C. To help other road users know what you intend to do
- D. To allow drivers to pass you on the right

58 At which type of crossing are cyclists allowed to ride across with pedestrians?

Mark one answer

- A. Toucan
- B. Puffin
- C. Pelican
- D. Zebra

59 A bus has stopped at a bus stop ahead of you. Its right-hand indicator is flashing. You should

Mark one answer

- A. flash your headlights and slow down
- B. slow down and give way if it is safe to do so
- C. sound your horn and keep going
- D. slow down and then sound your horn

60 You are travelling at the legal speed limit. A vehicle comes up quickly behind, flashing its headlights. You should

Mark one answer

- A. accelerate to make a gap behind you
- B. touch the brakes sharply to show your brake lights
- C. maintain your speed to prevent the vehicle from overtaking
- D. allow the vehicle to overtake

61 You should ONLY flash your headlights to other road users

Mark one answer

- A. to show that you are giving way
- B. to show that you are about to turn
- C. to tell them that you have right of way
- D. to let them know that you are there

62 You are approaching unmarked crossroads. How should you deal with this type of junction?

Mark one answer
- **A.** Accelerate and keep to the middle
- **B.** Slow down and keep to the right
- **C.** Accelerate looking to the left
- **D.** Slow down and look both ways

63 You are approaching a pelican crossing. The amber light is flashing. You must

Mark one answer
- **A.** give way to pedestrians who are crossing
- **B.** encourage pedestrians to cross
- **C.** not move until the green light appears
- **D.** stop even if the crossing is clear

64 At puffin crossings, which light will not show to a driver?

Mark one answer
- **A.** Flashing amber
- **B.** Red
- **C.** Steady amber
- **D.** Green

65 You should leave at least a two-second gap between your vehicle and the one in front when conditions are

Mark one answer
- **A.** wet
- **B.** good
- **C.** damp
- **D.** foggy

66 You are driving on a clear night. There is a steady stream of oncoming traffic. The national speed limit applies. Which lights should you use?

Mark one answer
- **A.** Full beam headlights
- **B.** Sidelights
- **C.** Dipped headlights
- **D.** Fog lights

67 You are driving behind a large goods vehicle. It signals left but steers to the right. You should

Mark one answer
- **A.** slow down and let the vehicle turn
- **B.** drive on, keeping to the left
- **C.** overtake on the right of it
- **D.** hold your speed and sound your horn

68 You are driving along this road. The red van cuts in close in front of you. What should you do?

Mark one answer
- **A.** Accelerate to get closer to the red van
- **B.** Give a long blast on the horn
- **C.** Drop back to leave the correct separation distance
- **D.** Flash your headlights several times

69 You are waiting in a traffic queue at night. To avoid dazzling following drivers you should

Mark one answer

- [ ] **A.** apply the handbrake only
- [ ] **B.** apply the footbrake only
- [ ] **C.** switch off your headlights
- [ ] **D.** use both the handbrake and footbrake

70 You are driving in traffic at the speed limit for the road. The driver behind is trying to overtake. You should

Mark one answer

- [ ] **A.** move closer to the car ahead, so the driver behind has no room to overtake
- [ ] **B.** wave the driver behind to overtake when it is safe
- [ ] **C.** keep a steady course and allow the driver behind to overtake
- [ ] **D.** accelerate to get away from the driver behind

71 You are driving at night on an unlit road behind another vehicle. You should

Mark one answer

- [ ] **A.** flash your headlights
- [ ] **B.** use dipped beam headlights
- [ ] **C.** switch off your headlights
- [ ] **D.** use full beam headlights

72 A bus lane on your left shows no times of operation. This means it is

BUS
LANE

Mark one answer

- [ ] **A.** not in operation at all
- [ ] **B.** only in operation at peak times
- [ ] **C.** in operation 24 hours a day
- [ ] **D.** only in operation in daylight hours

73 You are driving along a country road. A horse and rider are approaching. What should you do?

Mark two answers

- [ ] **A.** Increase your speed
- [ ] **B.** Sound your horn
- [ ] **C.** Flash your headlights
- [ ] **D.** Drive slowly past
- [ ] **E.** Give plenty of room
- [ ] **F.** Rev your engine

74 A person herding sheep asks you to stop. You should

Mark one answer

- A. ignore them as they have no authority
- B. stop and switch off your engine
- C. continue on but drive slowly
- D. try and get past quickly

75 When overtaking a horse and rider you should

Mark one answer

- A. sound your horn as a warning
- B. go past as quickly as possible
- C. flash your headlights as a warning
- D. go past slowly and carefully

76 You are approaching a zebra crossing. Pedestrians are waiting to cross. You should

Mark one answer

- A. give way to the elderly and infirm only
- B. slow down and prepare to stop
- C. use your headlights to indicate they can cross
- D. wave at them to cross the road

77 You are driving a slow-moving vehicle on a narrow winding road. You should

Mark one answer

- A. keep well out to stop vehicles overtaking dangerously
- B. wave following vehicles past you if you think they can overtake quickly
- C. pull in safely when you can, to let following vehicles overtake
- D. give a left signal when it is safe for vehicles to overtake you

78 You have a loose filler cap on your diesel fuel tank. This will

Mark two answers

- A. waste fuel and money
- B. make roads slippery for other road users
- C. improve your vehicle's fuel consumption
- D. increase the level of exhaust emissions

79 To avoid spillage after refuelling, you should make sure that

Mark one answer

- A. your tank is only three-quarters full
- B. you have used a locking filler cap
- C. you check your fuel gauge is working
- D. your filler cap is securely fastened

80 A vehicle pulls out in front of you at a junction. What should you do?

Mark one answer

- A. Swerve past it and sound your horn
- B. Flash your headlights and drive up close behind
- C. Slow down and be ready to stop
- D. Accelerate past it immediately

81 You stop for pedestrians waiting to cross at a zebra crossing. They do not start to cross. What should you do?

Mark one answer

- A. Be patient and wait
- B. Sound your horn
- C. Carry on
- D. Wave them to cross

82 You are following this lorry. You should keep well back from it to

Mark one answer
- A. give you a good view of the road ahead
- B. stop following traffic from rushing through the junction
- C. prevent traffic behind you from overtaking
- D. allow you to hurry through the traffic lights if they change

83 You are approaching a red light at a puffin crossing. Pedestrians are on the crossing. The red light will stay on until

Mark one answer
- A. you start to edge forward on to the crossing
- B. the pedestrians have reached a safe position
- C. the pedestrians are clear of the front of your vehicle
- D. a driver from the opposite direction reaches the crossing

84 Which instrument panel warning light would show that headlights are on full beam?

Mark one answer
- A.
- B.
- C.
- D.

85 If your vehicle uses diesel fuel, take extra care when refuelling. Diesel fuel when spilt is

Mark one answer
- A. sticky
- B. odourless
- C. clear
- D. slippery

86 What style of driving causes increased risk to everyone?

Mark one answer
- A. Considerate
- B. Defensive
- C. Competitive
- D. Responsible

87 Young, inexperienced and newly qualified drivers can often be involved in crashes. This is due to

Mark one answer
- A. being too cautious at junctions
- B. driving in the middle of their lane
- C. showing off and being competitive
- D. staying within the speed limit

88 Which of these, if allowed to get low, could cause you to crash?

Mark one answer

- [ ] **A.** Anti-freeze level
- [ ] **B.** Brake fluid level
- [ ] **C.** Battery water level
- [ ] **D.** Radiator coolant level

89 Which TWO are badly affected if the tyres are under-inflated?

Mark two answers

- [ ] **A.** Braking
- [ ] **B.** Steering
- [ ] **C.** Changing gear
- [ ] **D.** Parking

90 Motor vehicles can harm the environment. This has resulted in

Mark three answers

- [ ] **A.** air pollution
- [ ] **B.** damage to buildings
- [ ] **C.** less risk to health
- [ ] **D.** improved public transport
- [ ] **E.** less use of electrical vehicles
- [ ] **F.** using up of natural resources

91 Excessive or uneven tyre wear can be caused by faults in which THREE of the following?

Mark three answers

- [ ] **A.** The gearbox
- [ ] **B.** The braking system
- [ ] **C.** The accelerator
- [ ] **D.** The exhaust system
- [ ] **E.** Wheel alignment
- [ ] **F.** The suspension

92 You must NOT sound your horn

Mark one answer

- [ ] **A.** between 10pm and 6am in a built-up area
- [ ] **B.** at any time in a built-up area
- [ ] **C.** between 11.30pm and 7am in a built-up area
- [ ] **D.** between 11.30pm and 6am on any road

93 The pictured vehicle is 'environmentally friendly' because it

Mark three answers

- [ ] **A.** reduces noise pollution
- [ ] **B.** uses diesel fuel
- [ ] **C.** uses electricity
- [ ] **D.** uses unleaded fuel
- [ ] **E.** reduces parking spaces
- [ ] **F.** reduces town traffic

94 Supertrams or Light Rapid Transit (LRT) systems are environmentally friendly because

Mark one answer

- [ ] **A.** they use diesel power
- [ ] **B.** they use quieter roads
- [ ] **C.** they use electric power
- [ ] **D.** they do not operate during rush hour

95 'Red routes' in major cities have been introduced to

Mark one answer

- [ ] **A.** raise the speed limits
- [ ] **B.** help the traffic flow
- [ ] **C.** provide better parking
- [ ] **D.** allow lorries to load more freely

96 Road humps, chicanes and narrowings are

Mark one answer

- [ ] **A.** always at major road works
- [ ] **B.** used to increase traffic speed
- [ ] **C.** at toll-bridge approaches only
- [ ] **D.** traffic calming measures

97 The purpose of a catalytic converter is to reduce

Mark one answer

- **A.** fuel consumption
- **B.** the risk of fire
- **C.** toxic exhaust gases
- **D.** engine wear

98 Catalytic converters are fitted to make the

Mark one answer

- **A.** engine produce more power
- **B.** exhaust system easier to replace
- **C.** engine run quietly
- **D.** exhaust fumes cleaner

99 It is essential that tyre pressures are checked regularly. When should this be done?

Mark one answer

- **A.** After any lengthy journey
- **B.** After travelling at high speed
- **C.** When tyres are hot
- **D.** When tyres are cold

100 When should you NOT use your horn in a built-up area?

Mark one answer

- **A.** Between 8pm and 8am
- **B.** Between 9pm and dawn
- **C.** Between dusk and 8am
- **D.** Between 11.30pm and 7am

101 You will use more fuel if your tyres are

Mark one answer

- **A.** under-inflated
- **B.** of different makes
- **C.** over-inflated
- **D.** new and hardly used

102 How should you dispose of a used battery?

Mark two answers

- **A.** Take it to a local authority site
- **B.** Put it in the dustbin
- **C.** Break it up into pieces
- **D.** Leave it on waste land
- **E.** Take it to a garage
- **F.** Burn it on a fire

103 What is most likely to cause high fuel consumption?

Mark one answer

- **A.** Poor steering control
- **B.** Accelerating around bends
- **C.** Staying in high gears
- **D.** Harsh braking and accelerating

104 The fluid level in your battery is low. What should you top it up with?

Mark one answer

- **A.** Battery acid
- **B.** Distilled water
- **C.** Engine oil
- **D.** Engine coolant

105 You need to top up your battery. What level should you fill to?

Mark one answer

- **A.** The top of the battery
- **B.** Half-way up the battery
- **C.** Just below the cell plates
- **D.** Just above the cell plates

106 You have too much oil in your engine. What could this cause?

Mark one answer

- **A.** Low oil pressure
- **B.** Engine overheating
- **C.** Chain wear
- **D.** Oil leaks

107 You are parking on a two-way road at night. The speed limit is 40mph. You should park on the

Mark one answer
- [ ] **A.** left with parking lights on
- [ ] **B.** left with no lights on
- [ ] **C.** right with parking lights on
- [ ] **D.** right with dipped headlights on

108 You are parked on the road at night. Where must you use parking lights?

Mark one answer
- [ ] **A.** Where there are continuous white lines in the middle of the road
- [ ] **B.** Where the speed limit exceeds 30mph
- [ ] **C.** Where you are facing oncoming traffic
- [ ] **D.** Where you are near a bus stop

109 New petrol-engined cars must be fitted with catalytic converters. The reason for this is to

Mark one answer
- [ ] **A.** control exhaust noise levels
- [ ] **B.** prolong the life of the exhaust system
- [ ] **C.** allow the exhaust system to be recycled
- [ ] **D.** reduce harmful exhaust emissions

110 What can cause heavy steering?

Mark one answer
- [ ] **A.** Driving on ice
- [ ] **B.** Badly worn brakes
- [ ] **C.** Over-inflated tyres
- [ ] **D.** Under-inflated tyres

111 Driving with under-inflated tyres can affect

Mark two answers
- [ ] **A.** engine temperature
- [ ] **B.** fuel consumption
- [ ] **C.** braking
- [ ] **D.** oil pressure

112 Excessive or uneven tyre wear can be caused by faults in the

Mark two answers
- [ ] **A.** gearbox
- [ ] **B.** braking system
- [ ] **C.** suspension
- [ ] **D.** exhaust system

113 The main cause of brake fade is

Mark one answer
- [ ] **A.** the brakes overheating
- [ ] **B.** air in the brake fluid
- [ ] **C.** oil on the brakes
- [ ] **D.** the brakes out of adjustment

114 Your anti-lock brakes warning light stays on. You should

Mark one answer
- [ ] **A.** check the brake fluid level
- [ ] **B.** check the footbrake free play
- [ ] **C.** check that the handbrake is released
- [ ] **D.** have the brakes checked immediately

115 While driving, this warning light on your dashboard comes on. It means

Mark one answer
- [ ] **A.** a fault in the braking system
- [ ] **B.** the engine oil is low
- [ ] **C.** a rear light has failed
- [ ] **D.** your seat belt is not fastened

116 It is important to wear suitable shoes when you are driving. Why is this?

Mark one answer

- A. To prevent wear on the pedals
- B. To maintain control of the pedals
- C. To enable you to adjust your seat
- D. To enable you to walk for assistance if you break down

117 The most important reason for having a properly adjusted head restraint is to

Mark one answer

- A. make you more comfortable
- B. help you to avoid neck injury
- C. help you to relax
- D. help you to maintain your driving position

118 What will reduce the risk of neck injury resulting from a collision?

Mark one answer

- A. An air-sprung seat
- B. Anti-lock brakes
- C. A collapsible steering wheel
- D. A properly adjusted head restraint

119 You are driving the children of a friend home from school. They are both under 14 years old. Who is responsible for making sure they wear a seat belt or approved child restraint where required?

Mark one answer

- A. An adult passenger
- B. The children
- C. You, the driver
- D. Your friend

120 Car passengers MUST wear a seat belt/restraint if one is available, unless they are

Mark one answer

- A. under 14 years old
- B. under 1.5 metres (5 feet) in height
- C. sitting in the rear seat
- D. exempt for medical reasons

121 You are testing your suspension. You notice that your vehicle keeps bouncing when you press down on the front wing. What does this mean?

Mark one answer

- A. Worn tyres
- B. Tyres under-inflated
- C. Steering wheel not located centrally
- D. Worn shock absorbers

122 A roof rack fitted to your car will

Mark one answer

- A. reduce fuel consumption
- B. improve the road handling
- C. make your car go faster
- D. increase fuel consumption

123 It is illegal to drive with tyres that

Mark one answer

- A. have been bought second-hand
- B. have a large deep cut in the side wall
- C. are of different makes
- D. are of different tread patterns

124 The legal minimum depth of tread for car tyres over three quarters of the breadth is

Mark one answer

- A. 1mm
- B. 1.6mm
- C. 2.5mm
- D. 4mm

125 You are carrying two 13-year-old children and their parents in your car. Who is responsible for seeing that the children wear seat belts?

Mark one answer

- A. The children's parents
- B. You, the driver
- C. The front-seat passenger
- D. The children

126 When a roof rack is not in use it should be removed. Why is this?

Mark one answer

- A. It will affect the suspension
- B. It is illegal
- C. It will affect your braking
- D. It will waste fuel

127 How can you, as a driver, help the environment?

Mark three answers

- A. By reducing your speed
- B. By gentle acceleration
- C. By using leaded fuel
- D. By driving faster
- E. By harsh acceleration
- F. By servicing your vehicle properly

128 To help the environment, you can avoid wasting fuel by

Mark three answers

- A. having your vehicle properly serviced
- B. making sure your tyres are correctly inflated
- C. not over-revving in the lower gears
- D. driving at higher speeds where possible
- E. keeping an empty roof rack properly fitted
- F. servicing your vehicle less regularly

129 To reduce the volume of traffic on the roads you could

Mark three answers

- A. use public transport more often
- B. share a car when possible
- C. walk or cycle on short journeys
- D. travel by car at all times
- E. use a car with a smaller engine
- F. drive in a bus lane

130 Which THREE of the following are most likely to waste fuel?

Mark three answers

- A. Reducing your speed
- B. Carrying unnecessary weight
- C. Using the wrong grade of fuel
- D. Under-inflated tyres
- E. Using different brands of fuel
- F. A fitted, empty roof rack

131 Which THREE things can you, as a road user, do to help the environment?

Mark three answers

- A. Cycle when possible
- B. Drive on under-inflated tyres
- C. Use the choke for as long as possible on a cold engine
- D. Have your vehicle properly tuned and serviced
- E. Watch the traffic and plan ahead
- F. Brake as late as possible without skidding

132 As a driver you can cause more damage to the environment by

Mark two answers

- A. choosing a fuel-efficient vehicle
- B. making a lot of short journeys
- C. driving in as high a gear as possible
- D. accelerating as quickly as possible
- E. having your vehicle regularly serviced

133 To help protect the environment you should NOT

Mark one answer

- A. remove your roof rack when unloaded
- B. use your car for very short journeys
- C. walk, cycle or use public transport
- D. empty the boot of unnecessary weight

134 Which THREE does the law require you to keep in good condition?

Mark three answers
- A. Gears
- B. Transmission
- C. Headlights
- D. Windscreen
- E. Seat belts

135 Driving at 70mph uses more fuel than driving at 50mph by up to

Mark one answer
- A. 10%
- B. 30%
- C. 75%
- D. 100%

136 Your vehicle pulls to one side when braking. You should

Mark one answer
- A. change the tyres around
- B. consult your garage as soon as possible
- C. pump the pedal when braking
- D. use your handbrake at the same time

137 As a driver, you can help reduce pollution levels in town centres by

Mark one answer
- A. driving more quickly
- B. over-revving in a low gear
- C. walking or cycling
- D. driving short journeys

138 Unbalanced wheels on a car may cause

Mark one answer
- A. the steering to pull to one side
- B. the steering to vibrate
- C. the brakes to fail
- D. the tyres to deflate

139 Turning the steering wheel while your car is stationary can cause damage to the

Mark two answers
- A. gearbox
- B. engine
- C. brakes
- D. steering
- E. tyres

140 How can you reduce the chances of your car being broken into when leaving it unattended?

Mark one answer
- A. Take all valuables with you
- B. Park near a taxi rank
- C. Place any valuables on the floor
- D. Park near a fire station

141 You have to leave valuables in your car. It would be safer to

Mark one answer
- A. put them in a carrier bag
- B. park near a school entrance
- C. lock them out of sight
- D. park near a bus stop

142 How could you deter theft from your car when leaving it unattended?

Mark one answer
- A. Leave valuables in a carrier bag
- B. Lock valuables out of sight
- C. Put valuables on the seats
- D. Leave valuables on the floor

143 Which of the following may help to deter a thief from stealing your car?

Mark one answer
- A. Always keeping the headlights on
- B. Fitting reflective glass windows
- C. Always keeping the interior light on
- D. Etching the car number on the windows

144 How can you help to prevent your car radio being stolen?

Mark one answer

- A. Park in an unlit area
- B. Hide the radio with a blanket
- C. Park near a busy junction
- D. Install a security-coded radio

145 Which of the following should not be kept in your vehicle?

Mark one answer

- A. A first aid kit
- B. A road atlas
- C. The tax disc
- D. The vehicle documents

146 What should you do when leaving your vehicle?

Mark one answer

- A. Put valuable documents under the seats
- B. Remove all valuables
- C. Cover valuables with a blanket
- D. Leave the interior light on

147 You are parking your car. You have some valuables which you are unable to take with you. What should you do?

Mark one answer

- A. Park near a police station
- B. Put them under the driver's seat
- C. Lock them out of sight
- D. Park in an unlit side road

148 Which of these is most likely to deter the theft of your vehicle?

Mark one answer

- A. An immobiliser
- B. Tinted windows
- C. Locking wheel nuts
- D. A sun screen

149 Wherever possible, which one of the following should you do when parking at night?

Mark one answer

- A. Park in a quiet car park
- B. Park in a well-lit area
- C. Park facing against the flow of traffic
- D. Park next to a busy junction

150 When parking and leaving your car you should

Mark one answer

- A. park under a shady tree
- B. remove the tax disc
- C. park in a quiet road
- D. engage the steering lock

151 When leaving your vehicle parked and unattended you should

Mark one answer

- A. park near a busy junction
- B. park in a housing estate
- C. remove the key and lock it
- D. leave the left indicator on

152 How can you lessen the risk of your vehicle being broken into at night?

Mark one answer

- A. Leave it in a well-lit area
- B. Park in a quiet side road
- C. Don't engage the steering lock
- D. Park in a poorly-lit area

153 To help keep your car secure you could join a

Mark one answer

- A. vehicle breakdown organisation
- B. vehicle watch scheme
- C. advanced driver's scheme
- D. car maintenance class

154 Which TWO of the following will improve fuel consumption?

Mark two answers

- [ ] A. Reducing your road speed
- [ ] B. Planning well ahead
- [ ] C. Late and harsh braking
- [ ] D. Driving in lower gears
- [ ] E. Short journeys with a cold engine
- [ ] F. Rapid acceleration

155 You service your own vehicle. How should you get rid of the old engine oil?

Mark one answer

- [ ] A. Take it to a local authority site
- [ ] B. Pour it down a drain
- [ ] C. Tip it into a hole in the ground
- [ ] D. Put it into your dustbin

156 On a vehicle, where would you find a catalytic converter?

Mark one answer

- [ ] A. In the fuel tank
- [ ] B. In the air filter
- [ ] C. On the cooling system
- [ ] D. On the exhaust system

157 Why do MOT tests include a strict exhaust emission test?

Mark one answer

- [ ] A. To recover the cost of expensive garage equipment
- [ ] B. To help protect the environment against pollution
- [ ] C. To discover which fuel supplier is used the most
- [ ] D. To make sure diesel and petrol engines emit the same fumes

158 To reduce the damage your vehicle causes to the environment you should

Mark three answers

- [ ] A. use narrow side streets
- [ ] B. avoid harsh acceleration
- [ ] C. brake in good time
- [ ] D. anticipate well ahead
- [ ] E. use busy routes

159 Your vehicle has a catalytic converter. Its purpose is to reduce

Mark one answer

- [ ] A. exhaust noise
- [ ] B. fuel consumption
- [ ] C. exhaust emissions
- [ ] D. engine noise

160 A properly serviced vehicle will give

Mark two answers

- [ ] A. lower insurance premiums
- [ ] B. you a refund on your road tax
- [ ] C. better fuel economy
- [ ] D. cleaner exhaust emissions

161 You enter a road where there are road humps. What should you do?

Mark one answer

- [ ] A. Maintain a reduced speed throughout
- [ ] B. Accelerate quickly between each one
- [ ] C. Always keep to the maximum legal speed
- [ ] D. Drive slowly at school times only

162 When should you especially check the engine oil level?

Mark one answer
- A. Before a long journey
- B. When the engine is hot
- C. Early in the morning
- D. Every 6,000 miles

163 You are having difficulty finding a parking space in a busy town. You can see there is space on the zigzag lines of a zebra crossing. Can you park there?

Mark one answer
- A. No, unless you stay with your car
- B. Yes, in order to drop off a passenger
- C. Yes, if you do not block people from crossing
- D. No, not in any circumstances

164 When leaving your car unattended for a few minutes you should

Mark one answer
- A. leave the engine running
- B. switch the engine off but leave the key in
- C. lock it and remove the key
- D. park near a traffic warden

165 When parking and leaving your car for a few minutes you should

Mark one answer
- A. leave it unlocked
- B. lock it and remove the key
- C. leave the hazard warning lights on
- D. leave the interior light on

166 When leaving your car to help keep it secure you should

Mark one answer
- A. leave the hazard warning lights on
- B. lock it and remove the key
- C. park on a one-way street
- D. park in a residential area

167 When leaving your vehicle where should you park if possible?

Mark one answer
- A. Opposite a traffic island
- B. In a secure car park
- C. On a bend
- D. At or near a taxi rank

168 You are leaving your vehicle parked on a road unattended. When may you leave the engine running?

Mark one answer
- A. If you will be parking for less than 5 minutes
- B. If the battery keeps going flat
- C. When parked in a 20mph zone
- D. Never if you are away from the vehicle

169 In which THREE places would parking your vehicle cause danger or obstruction to other road users?

Mark three answers
- A. In front of a property entrance
- B. At or near a bus stop
- C. On your driveway
- D. In a marked parking space
- E. On the approach to a level crossing

170 In which THREE places would parking cause an obstruction to others?

Mark three answers
- A. Near the brow of a hill
- B. In a lay-by
- C. Where the kerb is raised
- D. Where the kerb has been lowered for wheelchairs
- E. At or near a bus stop

171 You are away from home and have to park your vehicle overnight. Where should you leave it?

Mark one answer
- A. Opposite another parked vehicle
- B. In a quiet road
- C. Opposite a traffic island
- D. In a secure car park

172 Before starting a journey it is wise to plan your route. How can you do this?

Mark one answer
- A. Look at a map
- B. Contact your local garage
- C. Look in your vehicle handbook
- D. Check your vehicle registration document

173 It can help to plan your route before starting a journey. You can do this by contacting

Mark one answer
- A. your local filling station   **NI**
- B. a motoring organisation
- C. the Driver Vehicle Licensing Agency
- D. your vehicle manufacturer

174 How can you plan your route before starting a long journey?

Mark one answer
- A. Check your vehicle's workshop manual
- B. Ask your local garage
- C. Use a route planner on the internet
- D. Consult your travel agents

175 Planning your route before setting out can be helpful. How can you do this?

Mark one answer
- A. Look in a motoring magazine
- B. Only visit places you know
- C. Try to travel at busy times
- D. Print or write down the route

176 Why is it a good idea to plan your journey to avoid busy times?

Mark one answer
- A. You will have an easier journey
- B. You will have a more stressful journey
- C. Your journey time will be longer
- D. It will cause more traffic congestion

177 Planning your journey to avoid busy times has a number of advantages. One of these is

Mark one answer
- A. your journey will take longer
- B. you will have a more pleasant journey
- C. you will cause more pollution
- D. your stress level will be greater

178 It is a good idea to plan your journey to avoid busy times. This is because

Mark one answer
- A. your vehicle will use more fuel
- B. you will see less road works
- C. it will help to ease congestion
- D. you will travel a much shorter distance

179 By avoiding busy times when travelling

Mark one answer
- A. you are more likely to be held up
- B. your journey time will be longer
- C. you will travel a much shorter distance
- D. you are less likely to be delayed

180 It can help to plan your route before starting a journey. Why should you also plan an alternative route?

Mark one answer
- A. Your original route may be blocked
- B. Your maps may have different scales
- C. You may find you have to pay a congestion charge
- D. Because you may get held up by a tractor

181 You will find that driving smoothly can

Mark one answer
- [ ] **A.** reduce journey times by about 15%
- [ ] **B.** increase fuel consumption by about 15%
- [ ] **C.** reduce fuel consumption by about 15%
- [ ] **D.** increase journey times by about 15%

182 You can save fuel when conditions allow by

Mark one answer
- [ ] **A.** using lower gears as often as possible
- [ ] **B.** accelerating sharply in each gear
- [ ] **C.** using each gear in turn
- [ ] **D.** missing out some gears

183 As well as planning your route before starting a journey, you should also plan an alternative route. Why is this?

Mark one answer
- [ ] **A.** To let another driver overtake
- [ ] **B.** Your first route may be blocked
- [ ] **C.** To avoid a railway level crossing
- [ ] **D.** In case you have to avoid emergency vehicles

184 You are making an appointment and will have to travel a long distance. You should

Mark one answer
- [ ] **A.** allow plenty of time for your journey
- [ ] **B.** plan to go at busy times
- [ ] **C.** avoid all national speed limit roads
- [ ] **D.** prevent other drivers from overtaking

185 You are checking your trailer tyres. What is the legal minimum tread depth over the central three quarters of its breadth?

Mark one answer
- [ ] **A.** 1mm
- [ ] **B.** 1.6mm
- [ ] **C.** 2mm
- [ ] **D.** 2.6mm

186 How can driving in an Eco-safe manner help protect the environment?

Mark one answer
- [ ] **A.** Through the legal enforcement of speed regulations
- [ ] **B.** By increasing the number of cars on the road
- [ ] **C.** Through increased fuel bills
- [ ] **D.** By reducing exhaust emissions

187 What does Eco-safe driving achieve?

Mark one answer
- [ ] **A.** Increased fuel consumption
- [ ] **B.** Improved road safety
- [ ] **C.** Damage to the environment
- [ ] **D.** Increased exhaust emissions

188 How can missing out some gear changes save fuel?

Mark one answer
- [ ] **A.** By reducing the amount of time you are accelerating
- [ ] **B.** Because there is less need to use the footbrake
- [ ] **C.** By controlling the amount of steering
- [ ] **D.** Because coasting is kept to a minimum

189 Fuel consumption is at its highest when you are

Mark one answer
- [ ] **A.** braking
- [ ] **B.** coasting
- [ ] **C.** accelerating
- [ ] **D.** steering

190 Missing out some gears saves fuel by reducing the amount of time you spend

Mark one answer
- [ ] **A.** braking
- [ ] **B.** coasting
- [ ] **C.** steering
- [ ] **D.** accelerating

191 Rapid acceleration and heavy braking can lead to

Mark one answer

- [ ] A. reduced pollution
- [ ] B. increased fuel consumption
- [ ] C. reduced exhaust emissions
- [ ] D. increased road safety

192 What percentage of all emissions does road transport account for?

Mark one answer

- [ ] A. 10%
- [ ] B. 20%
- [ ] C. 30%
- [ ] D. 40%

193 Car passengers MUST wear a seat belt if one is available, unless they are

Mark one answer

- [ ] A. in a vehicle fitted with air bags
- [ ] B. travelling within a congestion charging zone
- [ ] C. sitting in the rear seat
- [ ] D. exempt for medical reasons

194 You are carrying a 5-year-old child in the back seat of your car. They are under 1.35 metres (4 feet 5 inches) in height. A correct child restraint is NOT available. They MUST

Mark one answer

- [ ] A. sit behind the passenger seat
- [ ] B. use an adult seat belt
- [ ] C. share a belt with an adult
- [ ] D. sit between two other children

195 You are carrying a child using a rear-facing baby seat. You want to put it on the front passenger seat. What MUST you do before setting off?

Mark one answer

- [ ] A. Deactivate all front and rear airbags
- [ ] B. Make sure any front passenger airbag is deactivated
- [ ] C. Make sure all the child safety locks are off
- [ ] D. Recline the front passenger seat

196 You are carrying an 11-year-old child in the back seat of your car. They are under 1.35 metres (4 feet 5 inches) in height. You MUST make sure that

Mark one answer

- [ ] A. they sit between two belted people
- [ ] B. they can fasten their own seat belt
- [ ] C. a suitable child restraint is available
- [ ] D. they can see clearly out of the front window

197 You are parked at the side of the road. You will be waiting for some time for a passenger. What should you do?

Mark one answer

- [ ] A. Switch off the engine
- [ ] B. Apply the steering lock
- [ ] C. Switch off the radio
- [ ] D. Use your headlights

198 You are using a rear-facing baby seat. You want to put it on the front passenger seat which is protected by a frontal airbag. What MUST you do before setting off?

Mark one answer

- [ ] A. Deactivate the airbag
- [ ] B. Turn the seat to face sideways
- [ ] C. Ask a passenger to hold the baby
- [ ] D. Put the child in an adult seat belt

199 You are carrying a 5-year-old child in the back seat of your car. They are under 1.35 metres (4 feet 5 inches) in height. They MUST use an adult seat belt ONLY if

Mark one answer

- [ ] A. a correct child restraint is not available
- [ ] B. it is a lap type belt
- [ ] C. they sit between two adults
- [ ] D. it can be shared with another adult

200 Braking distances on ice can be

Mark one answer

- **A.** twice the normal distance
- **B.** five times the normal distance
- **C.** seven times the normal distance
- **D.** ten times the normal distance

201 Freezing conditions will affect the distance it takes you to come to a stop. You should expect stopping distances to increase by up to

Mark one answer

- **A.** two times
- **B.** three times
- **C.** five times
- **D.** ten times

202 In very hot weather the road surface can become soft. Which TWO of the following will be most affected?

Mark two answers

- **A.** The suspension
- **B.** The grip of the tyres
- **C.** The braking
- **D.** The exhaust

203 Where are you most likely to be affected by a side wind?

Mark one answer

- **A.** On a narrow country lane
- **B.** On an open stretch of road
- **C.** On a busy stretch of road
- **D.** On a long, straight road

204 In windy conditions you need to take extra care when

Mark one answer

- **A.** using the brakes
- **B.** making a hill start
- **C.** turning into a narrow road
- **D.** passing pedal cyclists

205 In good conditions, what is the typical stopping distance at 70mph?

Mark one answer

- **A.** 53 metres (175 feet)
- **B.** 60 metres (197 feet)
- **C.** 73 metres (240 feet)
- **D.** 96 metres (315 feet)

206 What is the shortest overall stopping distance on a dry road at 60mph?

Mark one answer

- **A.** 53 metres (175 feet)
- **B.** 58 metres (190 feet)
- **C.** 73 metres (240 feet)
- **D.** 96 metres (315 feet)

207 You are following a vehicle at a safe distance on a wet road. Another driver overtakes you and pulls into the gap you have left. What should you do?

Mark one answer

- **A.** Flash your headlights as a warning
- **B.** Try to overtake safely as soon as you can
- **C.** Drop back to regain a safe distance
- **D.** Stay close to the other vehicle until it moves on

208 When approaching a right-hand bend you should keep well to the left. Why is this?

Mark one answer

- **A.** To improve your view of the road
- **B.** To overcome the effect of the road's slope
- **C.** To let faster traffic from behind overtake
- **D.** To be positioned safely if you skid

209 You have just gone through deep water. To dry off the brakes you should

Mark one answer

- A. accelerate and keep to a high speed for a short time
- B. go slowly while gently applying the brakes
- C. avoid using the brakes at all for a few miles
- D. stop for at least an hour to allow them time to dry

210 You are on a fast, open road in good conditions. For safety, the distance between you and the vehicle in front should be

Mark one answer

- A. a two-second time gap
- B. one car length
- C. 2 metres (6 feet 6 inches)
- D. two car lengths

211 What is the most common cause of skidding?

Mark one answer

- A. Worn tyres
- B. Driver error
- C. Other vehicles
- D. Pedestrians

212 You are driving on an icy road. How can you avoid wheelspin?

Mark one answer

- A. Drive at a slow speed in as high a gear as possible
- B. Use the handbrake if the wheels start to slip
- C. Brake gently and repeatedly
- D. Drive in a low gear at all times

213 Skidding is mainly caused by

Mark one answer

- A. the weather
- B. the driver
- C. the vehicle
- D. the road

214 You are driving in freezing conditions. What should you do when approaching a sharp bend?

Mark two answers

- A. Slow down before you reach the bend
- B. Gently apply your handbrake
- C. Firmly use your footbrake
- D. Coast into the bend
- E. Avoid sudden steering movements

215 You are turning left on a slippery road. The back of your vehicle slides to the right. You should

Mark one answer

- A. brake firmly and not turn the steering wheel
- B. steer carefully to the left
- C. steer carefully to the right
- D. brake firmly and steer to the left

216 Travelling for long distances in neutral (known as coasting)

Mark one answer

- A. improves the driver's control
- B. makes steering easier
- C. reduces the driver's control
- D. uses more fuel

217 Before starting a journey in freezing weather you should clear ice and snow from your vehicle's

Mark four answers

- [ ] A. aerial
- [ ] B. windows
- [ ] C. bumper
- [ ] D. lights
- [ ] E. mirrors
- [ ] F. number plates

218 You are trying to move off on snow. You should use

Mark one answer

- [ ] A. the lowest gear you can
- [ ] B. the highest gear you can
- [ ] C. a high engine speed
- [ ] D. the handbrake and footbrake together

219 When driving in falling snow you should

Mark one answer

- [ ] A. brake firmly and quickly
- [ ] B. be ready to steer sharply
- [ ] C. use sidelights only
- [ ] D. brake gently in plenty of time

220 The MAIN benefit of having four-wheel drive is to improve

Mark one answer

- [ ] A. road holding
- [ ] B. fuel consumption
- [ ] C. stopping distances
- [ ] D. passenger comfort

221 You are about to go down a steep hill. To control the speed of your vehicle you should

Mark one answer

- [ ] A. select a high gear and use the brakes carefully
- [ ] B. select a high gear and use the brakes firmly
- [ ] C. select a low gear and use the brakes carefully
- [ ] D. select a low gear and avoid using the brakes

222 How can you use your vehicle's engine as a brake?

Mark one answer

- [ ] A. By changing to a lower gear
- [ ] B. By selecting reverse gear
- [ ] C. By changing to a higher gear
- [ ] D. By selecting neutral gear

223 You wish to park facing DOWNHILL. Which TWO of the following should you do?

Mark two answers

- [ ] A. Turn the steering wheel towards the kerb
- [ ] B. Park close to the bumper of another car
- [ ] C. Park with two wheels on the kerb
- [ ] D. Put the handbrake on firmly
- [ ] E. Turn the steering wheel away from the kerb

224 You are driving in a built-up area. You approach a speed hump. You should

Mark one answer

- [ ] A. move across to the left-hand side of the road
- [ ] B. wait for any pedestrians to cross
- [ ] C. slow your vehicle right down
- [ ] D. stop and check both pavements

225 You are on a long, downhill slope. What should you do to help control the speed of your vehicle?

Mark one answer

- [ ] A. Select neutral
- [ ] B. Select a lower gear
- [ ] C. Grip the handbrake firmly
- [ ] D. Apply the parking brake gently

226 Your vehicle is fitted with anti-lock brakes. To stop quickly in an emergency you should

Mark one answer

- **A.** brake firmly and pump the brake pedal on and off
- **B.** brake rapidly and firmly without releasing the brake pedal
- **C.** brake gently and pump the brake pedal on and off
- **D.** brake rapidly once, and immediately release the brake pedal

227 Anti-lock brakes prevent wheels from locking. This means the tyres are less likely to

Mark one answer

- **A.** aquaplane
- **B.** skid
- **C.** puncture
- **D.** wear

228 Anti-lock brakes reduce the chances of a skid occurring particularly when

Mark one answer

- **A.** driving down steep hills
- **B.** braking during normal driving
- **C.** braking in an emergency
- **D.** driving on good road surfaces

229 Anti-lock brakes are most effective when you

Mark one answer

- **A.** keep pumping the footbrake to prevent skidding
- **B.** brake normally, but grip the steering wheel tightly
- **C.** brake promptly and firmly until you have slowed down
- **D.** apply the handbrake to reduce the stopping distance

230 Your car is fitted with anti-lock brakes. You need to stop in an emergency. You should

Mark one answer

- **A.** brake normally and avoid turning the steering wheel
- **B.** press the brake pedal promptly and firmly until you have stopped
- **C.** keep pushing and releasing the footbrake quickly to prevent skidding
- **D.** apply the handbrake to reduce the stopping distance

231 Vehicles fitted with anti-lock brakes

Mark one answer

- **A.** are impossible to skid
- **B.** can be steered while you are braking
- **C.** accelerate much faster
- **D.** are not fitted with a handbrake

232 Anti-lock brakes may not work as effectively if the road surface is

Mark two answers

- **A.** dry
- **B.** loose
- **C.** wet
- **D.** good
- **E.** firm

233 Anti-lock brakes are of most use when you are

Mark one answer

- **A.** braking gently
- **B.** driving on worn tyres
- **C.** braking excessively
- **D.** driving normally

234 Driving a vehicle fitted with anti-lock brakes allows you to

Mark one answer

- A. brake harder because it is impossible to skid
- B. drive at higher speeds
- C. steer and brake at the same time
- D. pay less attention to the road ahead

235 Anti-lock brakes can greatly assist with

Mark one answer

- A. a higher cruising speed
- B. steering control when braking
- C. control when accelerating
- D. motorway driving

236 When would an anti-lock braking system start to work?

Mark one answer

- A. After the parking brake has been applied
- B. Whenever pressure on the brake pedal is applied
- C. Just as the wheels are about to lock
- D. When the normal braking system fails to operate

237 You are driving a vehicle fitted with anti-lock brakes. You need to stop in an emergency. You should apply the footbrake

Mark one answer

- A. slowly and gently
- B. slowly but firmly
- C. rapidly and gently
- D. rapidly and firmly

238 Your vehicle has anti-lock brakes, but they may not always prevent skidding. This is most likely to happen when driving

Mark two answers

- A. in foggy conditions
- B. on surface water
- C. on loose road surfaces
- D. on dry tarmac
- E. at night on unlit roads

239 Anti-lock brakes will take effect when

Mark one answer

- A. you do not brake quickly enough
- B. maximum brake pressure has been applied
- C. you have not seen a hazard ahead
- D. speeding on slippery road surfaces

240 When driving in fog, which THREE of these are correct?

Mark three answers

- A. Use dipped headlights
- B. Position close to the centre line
- C. Allow more time for your journey
- D. Keep close to the car in front
- E. Slow down
- F. Use sidelights only

241 You are driving along a country road. You see this sign. AFTER dealing safely with the hazard you should always

Mark one answer

- A. check your tyre pressures
- B. switch on your hazard warning lights
- C. accelerate briskly
- D. test your brakes

242 You are driving in heavy rain. Your steering suddenly becomes very light. You should

Mark one answer

- A. steer towards the side of the road
- B. apply gentle acceleration
- C. brake firmly to reduce speed
- D. ease off the accelerator

243 How can you tell when you are driving over black ice?

Mark one answer

- A. It is easier to brake
- B. The noise from your tyres sounds louder
- C. You will see tyre tracks on the road
- D. Your steering feels light

244 The roads are icy. You should drive slowly

Mark one answer

- A. in the highest gear possible
- B. in the lowest gear possible
- C. with the handbrake partly on
- D. with your left foot on the brake

245 You are driving along a wet road. How can you tell if your vehicle is aquaplaning?

Mark one answer

- A. The engine will stall
- B. The engine noise will increase
- C. The steering will feel very heavy
- D. The steering will feel very light

246 How can you tell if you are driving on ice?

Mark two answers

- A. The tyres make a rumbling noise
- B. The tyres make hardly any noise
- C. The steering becomes heavier
- D. The steering becomes lighter

247 You are driving along a wet road. How can you tell if your vehicle's tyres are losing their grip on the surface?

Mark one answer

- A. The engine will stall
- B. The steering will feel very heavy
- C. The engine noise will increase
- D. The steering will feel very light

248 You are travelling at 50mph on a good, dry road. What is your typical overall stopping distance?

Mark one answer

- A. 36 metres (120 feet)
- B. 53 metres (175 feet)
- C. 75 metres (245 feet)
- D. 96 metres (315 feet)

249 Your overall stopping distance will be much longer when driving

Mark one answer

- A. in the rain
- B. in fog
- C. at night
- D. in strong winds

250 You have driven through a flood. What is the first thing you should do?

Mark one answer

- A. Stop and check the tyres
- B. Stop and dry the brakes
- C. Check your exhaust
- D. Test your brakes

251 Overall stopping distance is made up of thinking and braking distance. You are on a good, dry road surface with good brakes and tyres. What is a typical BRAKING distance from 50mph?

Mark one answer
- A. 14 metres (46 feet)
- B. 24 metres (80 feet)
- C. 38 metres (125 feet)
- D. 55 metres (180 feet)

252 You are on a good, dry road surface. Your brakes and tyres are good. What is the typical overall STOPPING distance at 40mph?

Mark one answer
- A. 23 metres (75 feet)
- B. 36 metres (120 feet)
- C. 53 metres (175 feet)
- D. 96 metres (315 feet)

253 You are on a wet motorway with surface spray. You should use

Mark one answer
- A. hazard flashers
- B. dipped headlights
- C. rear fog lights
- D. sidelights

254 What should you do when overtaking a motorcyclist in strong winds?

Mark one answer
- A. Pass close
- B. Pass quickly
- C. Pass wide
- D. Pass immediately

255 You are overtaking a motorcyclist in strong winds? What should you do?

Mark one answer
- A. Allow extra room
- B. Give a thank you wave
- C. Move back early
- D. Sound your horn

256 In heavy motorway traffic the vehicle behind you is following too closely. How can you lower the risk of a collision?

Mark one answer
- A. Increase your distance from the vehicle in front
- B. Operate the brakes sharply
- C. Switch on your hazard lights
- D. Move onto the hard shoulder and stop

257 You are following other vehicles in fog. You have your lights on. What else can you do to reduce the chances of being in a collision?

Mark one answer
- A. Keep close to the vehicle in front
- B. Use your main beam instead of dipped headlights
- C. Keep up with the faster vehicles
- D. Reduce your speed and increase the gap in front

258 To avoid a collision when entering a contraflow system, you should

Mark three answers
- A. reduce speed in good time
- B. switch lanes at any time to make progress
- C. choose an appropriate lane in good time
- D. keep the correct separation distance
- E. increase speed to pass through quickly
- F. follow other motorists closely to avoid long queues

259
You see this sign on the rear of a slow-moving lorry that you want to pass. It is travelling in the middle lane of a three-lane motorway. You should

Mark one answer

- [ ] **A.** cautiously approach the lorry then pass on either side
- [ ] **B.** follow the lorry until you can leave the motorway
- [ ] **C.** wait on the hard shoulder until the lorry has stopped
- [ ] **D.** approach with care and keep to the left of the lorry

260
Where would you expect to see these markers?

Mark two answers

- [ ] **A.** On a motorway sign
- [ ] **B.** At the entrance to a narrow bridge
- [ ] **C.** On a large goods vehicle
- [ ] **D.** On a builder's skip placed on the road

261
What does this signal from a police officer mean to oncoming traffic?

Mark one answer

- [ ] **A.** Go ahead
- [ ] **B.** Stop
- [ ] **C.** Turn left
- [ ] **D.** Turn right

262
What is the main hazard shown in this picture?

Mark one answer

- [ ] **A.** Vehicles turning right
- [ ] **B.** Vehicles doing U-turns
- [ ] **C.** The cyclist crossing the road
- [ ] **D.** Parked cars around the corner

263 Which road user has caused a hazard?

Mark one answer
- A. The parked car (arrowed A)
- B. The pedestrian waiting to cross (arrowed B)
- C. The moving car (arrowed C)
- D. The car turning (arrowed D)

264 What should the driver of the car approaching the crossing do?

Mark one answer
- A. Continue at the same speed
- B. Sound the horn
- C. Drive through quickly
- D. Slow down and get ready to stop

265 What THREE things should the driver of the grey car (arrowed) be especially aware of?

Mark three answers
- A. Pedestrians stepping out between cars
- B. Other cars behind the grey car
- C. Doors opening on parked cars
- D. The bumpy road surface
- E. Cars leaving parking spaces
- F. Empty parking spaces

266 You think the driver of the vehicle in front has forgotten to cancel their right indicator. You should

Mark one answer
- A. flash your lights to alert the driver
- B. sound your horn before overtaking
- C. overtake on the left if there is room
- D. stay behind and not overtake

267 What is the main hazard the driver of the red car (arrowed) should be aware of?

Mark one answer
- [ ] **A.** Glare from the sun may affect the driver's vision
- [ ] **B.** The black car may stop suddenly
- [ ] **C.** The bus may move out into the road
- [ ] **D.** Oncoming vehicles will assume the driver is turning right

268 You see this sign ahead. You should expect the road to

Mark one answer
- [ ] **A.** go steeply uphill
- [ ] **B.** go steeply downhill
- [ ] **C.** bend sharply to the left
- [ ] **D.** bend sharply to the right

269 You are approaching this cyclist. You should

Mark one answer
- [ ] **A.** overtake before the cyclist gets to the junction
- [ ] **B.** flash your headlights at the cyclist
- [ ] **C.** slow down and allow the cyclist to turn
- [ ] **D.** overtake the cyclist on the left-hand side

270 Why must you take extra care when turning right at this junction?

Mark one answer
- [ ] **A.** Road surface is poor
- [ ] **B.** Footpaths are narrow
- [ ] **C.** Road markings are faint
- [ ] **D.** There is reduced visibility

271 This yellow sign on a vehicle indicates this is

Mark one answer
- **A.** a broken-down vehicle
- **B.** a school bus
- **C.** an ice-cream van
- **D.** a private ambulance

272 When approaching this bridge you should give way to

Mark one answer
- **A.** bicycles
- **B.** buses
- **C.** motorcycles
- **D.** cars

273 What type of vehicle could you expect to meet in the middle of the road?

Mark one answer
- **A.** Lorry
- **B.** Bicycle
- **C.** Car
- **D.** Motorcycle

274 At this blind junction you must stop

Mark one answer
- **A.** behind the line, then edge forward to see clearly
- **B.** beyond the line at a point where you can see clearly
- **C.** only if there is traffic on the main road
- **D.** only if you are turning to the right

275
A driver pulls out of a side road in front of you. You have to brake hard. You should

Mark one answer

- A. ignore the error and stay calm
- B. flash your lights to show your annoyance
- C. sound your horn to show your annoyance
- D. overtake as soon as possible

276
An elderly person's driving ability could be affected because they may be unable to

Mark one answer

- A. obtain car insurance
- B. understand road signs
- C. react very quickly
- D. give signals correctly

277
You have just passed these warning lights. What hazard would you expect to see next?

Mark one answer

- A. A level crossing with no barrier
- B. An ambulance station
- C. A school crossing patrol
- D. An opening bridge

278
Why should you be especially cautious when going past this stationary bus?

Mark two answers

- A. There is traffic approaching in the distance
- B. The driver may open the door
- C. It may suddenly move off
- D. People may cross the road in front of it
- E. There are bicycles parked on the pavement

279
In areas where there are 'traffic calming' measures you should

Mark one answer

- A. travel at a reduced speed
- B. always travel at the speed limit
- C. position in the centre of the road
- D. only slow down if pedestrians are near

280
You are planning a long journey. Do you need to plan rest stops?

Mark one answer

- A. Yes, you should plan to stop every half an hour
- B. Yes, regular stops help concentration
- C. No, you will be less tired if you get there as soon as possible
- D. No, only fuel stops will be needed

281 A driver does something that upsets you. You should

Mark one answer

- [ ] A. try not to react
- [ ] B. let them know how you feel
- [ ] C. flash your headlights several times
- [ ] D. sound your horn

282 The red lights are flashing. What should you do when approaching this level crossing?

Mark one answer

- [ ] A. Go through quickly
- [ ] B. Go through carefully
- [ ] C. Stop before the barrier
- [ ] D. Switch on hazard warning lights

283 What TWO main hazards should you be aware of when going along this street?

Mark two answers

- [ ] A. Glare from the sun
- [ ] B. Car doors opening suddenly
- [ ] C. Lack of road markings
- [ ] D. The headlights on parked cars being switched on
- [ ] E. Large goods vehicles
- [ ] F. Children running out from between vehicles

284 What is the main hazard you should be aware of when following this cyclist?

Mark one answer

- [ ] A. The cyclist may move to the left and dismount
- [ ] B. The cyclist may swerve out into the road
- [ ] C. The contents of the cyclist's carrier may fall on to the road
- [ ] D. The cyclist may wish to turn right at the end of the road

285 When approaching this hazard why should you slow down?

Mark two answers

- **A.** Because of the bend
- **B.** Because it's hard to see to the right
- **C.** Because of approaching traffic
- **D.** Because of animals crossing
- **E.** Because of the level crossing

286 A driver's behaviour has upset you. It may help if you

Mark one answer

- **A.** stop and take a break
- **B.** shout abusive language
- **C.** gesture to them with your hand
- **D.** follow their car, flashing your headlights

287 You are on a dual carriageway. Ahead you see a vehicle with an amber flashing light. What will this be?

Mark one answer

- **A.** An ambulance
- **B.** A fire engine
- **C.** A doctor on call
- **D.** A disabled person's vehicle

288 You are approaching crossroads. The traffic lights have failed. What should you do?

Mark one answer

- **A.** Brake and stop only for large vehicles
- **B.** Brake sharply to a stop before looking
- **C.** Be prepared to brake sharply to a stop
- **D.** Be prepared to stop for any traffic

289 Why are place names painted on the road surface?

Mark one answer

- **A.** To restrict the flow of traffic
- **B.** To warn you of oncoming traffic
- **C.** To enable you to change lanes early
- **D.** To prevent you changing lanes

290 What should the driver of the red car (arrowed) do?

Mark one answer

- **A.** Wave the pedestrians who are waiting to cross
- **B.** Wait for the pedestrian in the road to cross
- **C.** Quickly drive behind the pedestrian in the road
- **D.** Tell the pedestrian in the road she should not have crossed

291

You are following a slower-moving vehicle on a narrow country road. There is a junction just ahead on the right. What should you do?

Mark one answer

- **A.** Overtake after checking your mirrors and signalling
- **B.** Stay behind until you are past the junction
- **C.** Accelerate quickly to pass before the junction
- **D.** Slow down and prepare to overtake on the left

292

What should you do as you approach this overhead bridge?

Mark one answer

- **A.** Move out to the centre of the road before going through
- **B.** Find another route, this is only for high vehicles
- **C.** Be prepared to give way to large vehicles in the middle of the road
- **D.** Move across to the right-hand side before going through

293

Why are mirrors often slightly curved (convex)?

Mark one answer

- **A.** They give a wider field of vision
- **B.** They totally cover blind spots
- **C.** They make it easier to judge the speed of following traffic
- **D.** They make following traffic look bigger

294

What does the solid white line at the side of the road indicate?

Mark one answer

- **A.** Traffic lights ahead
- **B.** Edge of the carriageway
- **C.** Footpath on the left
- **D.** Cycle path

295

You are driving towards this level crossing. What would be the first warning of an approaching train?

Mark one answer

- **A.** Both half barriers down
- **B.** A steady amber light
- **C.** One half barrier down
- **D.** Twin flashing red lights

296
You are driving along this motorway. It is raining. When following this lorry you should

Mark two answers
- **A.** allow at least a two-second gap
- **B.** move left and drive on the hard shoulder
- **C.** allow at least a four-second gap
- **D.** be aware of spray reducing your vision
- **E.** move right and stay in the right-hand lane

297
You are behind this cyclist. When the traffic lights change, what should you do?

Mark one answer
- **A.** Try to move off before the cyclist
- **B.** Allow the cyclist time and room
- **C.** Turn right but give the cyclist room
- **D.** Tap your horn and drive through first

298
You are driving towards this left-hand bend. What dangers should you be aware of?

Mark one answer
- **A.** A vehicle overtaking you
- **B.** No white lines in the centre of the road
- **C.** No sign to warn you of the bend
- **D.** Pedestrians walking towards you

299
While driving, you see this sign ahead. You should

Mark one answer
- **A.** stop at the sign
- **B.** slow, but continue around the bend
- **C.** slow to a crawl and continue
- **D.** stop and look for open farm gates

300 Why should the junction on the left be kept clear?

Mark one answer
- [ ] **A.** To allow vehicles to enter and emerge
- [ ] **B.** To allow the bus to reverse
- [ ] **C.** To allow vehicles to make a U-turn
- [ ] **D.** To allow vehicles to park

301 When the traffic lights change to green the white car should

Mark one answer
- [ ] **A.** wait for the cyclist to pull away
- [ ] **B.** move off quickly and turn in front of the cyclist
- [ ] **C.** move close up to the cyclist to beat the lights
- [ ] **D.** sound the horn to warn the cyclist

302 You intend to turn left at the traffic lights. Just before turning you should

Mark one answer
- [ ] **A.** check your right mirror
- [ ] **B.** move close up to the white car
- [ ] **C.** straddle the lanes
- [ ] **D.** check for bicycles on your left

303 You should reduce your speed when drving along this road because

Mark one answer
- [ ] **A.** there is a staggered junction ahead
- [ ] **B.** there is a low bridge ahead
- [ ] **C.** there is a change in the road surface
- [ ] **D.** the road ahead narrows

304 You are driving at 60mph. As you approach this hazard you should

Mark one answer
- [ ] **A.** maintain your speed
- [ ] **B.** reduce your speed
- [ ] **C.** take the next right turn
- [ ] **D.** take the next left turn

305 The traffic ahead of you in the left-hand lane is slowing. You should

Mark two answers
- [ ] **A.** be wary of cars on your right cutting in
- [ ] **B.** accelerate past the vehicles in the left-hand lane
- [ ] **C.** pull up on the left-hand verge
- [ ] **D.** move across and continue in the right-hand lane
- [ ] **E.** slow down, keeping a safe separation distance

306 What might you expect to happen in this situation?

Mark one answer
- [ ] **A.** Traffic will move into the right-hand lane
- [ ] **B.** Traffic speed will increase
- [ ] **C.** Traffic will move into the left-hand lane
- [ ] **D.** Traffic will not need to change position

307 You are driving on a road with several lanes. You see these signs above the lanes. What do they mean?

Mark one answer
- [ ] **A.** The two right lanes are open
- [ ] **B.** The two left lanes are open
- [ ] **C.** Traffic in the left lanes should stop
- [ ] **D.** Traffic in the right lanes should stop

308 As a provisional licence holder, you must not drive a motor car

Mark two answers

- A. at more than 40mph
- B. on your own
- C. on the motorway
- D. under the age of 18 years at night
- E. with passengers in the rear seats

309 After passing your driving test, you suffer from ill health. This affects your driving. You MUST

Mark one answer

- A. inform your local police station
- B. avoid using motorways
- C. always drive accompanied
- D. inform the licensing authority

310 You are invited to a pub lunch. You know that you will have to drive in the evening. What is your best course of action?

Mark one answer

- A. Avoid mixing your alcoholic drinks
- B. Not drink any alcohol at all
- C. Have some milk before drinking alcohol
- D. Eat a hot meal with your alcoholic drinks

311 You have been convicted of driving whilst unfit through drink or drugs. You will find this is likely to cause the cost of one of the following to rise considerably. Which one?

Mark one answer

- A. Road fund licence
- B. Insurance premiums
- C. Vehicle test certificate
- D. Driving licence

312 What advice should you give to a driver who has had a few alcoholic drinks at a party?

Mark one answer

- A. Have a strong cup of coffee and then drive home
- B. Drive home carefully and slowly
- C. Go home by public transport
- D. Wait a short while and then drive home

313 You have been taking medicine for a few days which made you feel drowsy. Today you feel better but still need to take the medicine. You should only drive

Mark one answer

- A. if your journey is necessary
- B. at night on quiet roads
- C. if someone goes with you
- D. after checking with your doctor

314
You are about to return home from holiday when you become ill. A doctor prescribes drugs which are likely to affect your driving. You should

Mark one answer
- A. drive only if someone is with you
- B. avoid driving on motorways
- C. not drive yourself
- D. never drive at more than 30mph

315
During periods of illness your ability to drive may be impaired. You MUST

Mark two answers
- A. see your doctor each time before you drive
- B. only take smaller doses of any medicines
- C. be medically fit to drive
- D. not drive after taking certain medicines
- E. take all your medicines with you when you drive

316
You feel drowsy when driving. You should

Mark two answers
- A. stop and rest as soon as possible
- B. turn the heater up to keep you warm and comfortable
- C. make sure you have a good supply of fresh air
- D. continue with your journey but drive more slowly
- E. close the car windows to help you concentrate

317
You are driving along a motorway and become tired. You should

Mark two answers
- A. stop at the next service area and rest
- B. leave the motorway at the next exit and rest
- C. increase your speed and turn up the radio volume
- D. close all your windows and set heating to warm
- E. pull up on the hard shoulder and change drivers

318
You are taking drugs that are likely to affect your driving. What should you do?

Mark one answer
- A. Seek medical advice before driving
- B. Limit your driving to essential journeys
- C. Only drive if accompanied by a full licence-holder
- D. Drive only for short distances

319
You are about to drive home. You feel very tired and have a severe headache. You should

Mark one answer
- A. wait until you are fit and well before driving
- B. drive home, but take a tablet for headaches
- C. drive home if you can stay awake for the journey
- D. wait for a short time, then drive home slowly

320 If you are feeling tired it is best to stop as soon as you can. Until then you should

Mark one answer

- [ ] **A.** increase your speed to find a stopping place quickly
- [ ] **B.** ensure a supply of fresh air
- [ ] **C.** gently tap the steering wheel
- [ ] **D.** keep changing speed to improve concentration

321 Your motorway journey seems boring and you feel drowsy. What should you do?

Mark one answer

- [ ] **A.** stop on the hard shoulder for a sleep
- [ ] **B.** open a window and stop as soon as it's safe and legal
- [ ] **C.** speed up to arrive at your destination sooner
- [ ] **D.** slow down and let other drivers overtake

322 Driving long distances can be tiring. You can prevent this by

Mark three answers

- [ ] **A.** stopping every so often for a walk
- [ ] **B.** opening a window for some fresh air
- [ ] **C.** ensuring plenty of refreshment breaks
- [ ] **D.** completing the journey without stopping
- [ ] **E.** eating a large meal before driving

323 You go to a social event and need to drive a short time after. What precaution should you take?

Mark one answer

- [ ] **A.** Avoid drinking alcohol on an empty stomach
- [ ] **B.** Drink plenty of coffee after drinking alcohol
- [ ] **C.** Avoid drinking alcohol completely
- [ ] **D.** Drink plenty of milk before drinking alcohol

324 You take some cough medicine given to you by a friend. What should you do before driving?

Mark one answer

- [ ] **A.** Ask your friend if taking the medicine affected their driving
- [ ] **B.** Drink some strong coffee one hour before driving
- [ ] **C.** Check the label to see if the medicine will affect your driving
- [ ] **D.** Drive a short distance to see if the medicine is affecting your driving

325 You take the wrong route and find you are on a one-way street. You should

Mark one answer

- [ ] **A.** reverse out of the road
- [ ] **B.** turn round in a side road
- [ ] **C.** continue to the end of the road
- [ ] **D.** reverse into a driveway

326 Which THREE are likely to make you lose concentration while driving?

Mark three answers

- [ ] A. Looking at road maps
- [ ] B. Listening to loud music
- [ ] C. Using your windscreen washers
- [ ] D. Looking in your wing mirror
- [ ] E. Using a mobile phone

327 You are driving along this road. The driver on the left is reversing from a driveway. You should

Mark one answer

- [ ] A. move to the opposite side of the road
- [ ] B. drive through as you have priority
- [ ] C. sound your horn and be prepared to stop
- [ ] D. speed up and drive through quickly

328 You have been involved in an argument before starting your journey. This has made you feel angry. You should

Mark one answer

- [ ] A. start to drive, but open a window
- [ ] B. drive slower than normal and turn your radio on
- [ ] C. have an alcoholic drink to help you relax before driving
- [ ] D. calm down before you start to drive

329 You start to feel tired while driving. What should you do?

Mark one answer

- [ ] A. Increase your speed slightly
- [ ] B. Decrease your speed slightly
- [ ] C. Find a less busy route
- [ ] D. Pull over at a safe place to rest

330 You are driving on this dual carriageway. Why may you need to slow down?

Mark one answer

- [ ] A. There is a broken white line in the centre
- [ ] B. There are solid white lines either side
- [ ] C. There are road works ahead of you
- [ ] D. There are no footpaths

331
You have just been overtaken by this motorcyclist who is cutting in sharply. You should

Mark one answer
- [ ] A. sound the horn
- [ ] B. brake firmly
- [ ] C. keep a safe gap
- [ ] D. flash your lights

332
You are about to drive home. You cannot find the glasses you need to wear. You should

Mark one answer
- [ ] A. drive home slowly, keeping to quiet roads
- [ ] B. borrow a friend's glasses and use those
- [ ] C. drive home at night, so that the lights will help you
- [ ] D. find a way of getting home without driving

333
Which THREE result from drinking alcohol?

Mark three answers
- [ ] A. Less control
- [ ] B. A false sense of confidence
- [ ] C. Faster reactions
- [ ] D. Poor judgement of speed
- [ ] E. Greater awareness of danger

334
Which THREE of these are likely effects of drinking alcohol?

Mark three answers
- [ ] A. Reduced co-ordination
- [ ] B. Increased confidence
- [ ] C. Poor judgement
- [ ] D. Increased concentration
- [ ] E. Faster reactions
- [ ] F. Colour blindness

335
How does alcohol affect you?

Mark one answer
- [ ] A. It speeds up your reactions
- [ ] B. It increases your awareness
- [ ] C. It improves your co-ordination
- [ ] D. It reduces your concentration

336
Your doctor has given you a course of medicine. Why should you ask how it will affect you?

Mark one answer
- [ ] A. Drugs make you a better driver by quickening your reactions
- [ ] B. You will have to let your insurance company know about the medicine
- [ ] C. Some types of medicine can cause your reactions to slow down
- [ ] D. The medicine you take may affect your hearing

337 You are not sure if your cough medicine will affect you. What TWO things should you do?

Mark two answers
- A. Ask your doctor
- B. Check the medicine label
- C. Drive if you feel alright
- D. Ask a friend or relative for advice

338 You are on a motorway. You feel tired. You should

Mark one answer
- A. carry on but go slowly
- B. leave the motorway at the next exit
- C. complete your journey as quickly as possible
- D. stop on the hard shoulder

339 You find that you need glasses to read vehicle number plates at the required distance. When MUST you wear them?

Mark one answer
- A. Only in bad weather conditions
- B. At all times when driving
- C. Only when you think it necessary
- D. Only in bad light or at night time

340 Which TWO things would help to keep you alert during a long journey?

Mark two answers
- A. Finishing your journey as fast as you can
- B. Keeping off the motorways and using country roads
- C. Making sure that you get plenty of fresh air
- D. Making regular stops for refreshments

341 Which of the following types of glasses should NOT be worn when driving at night?

Mark one answer
- A. Half-moon
- B. Round
- C. Bi-focal
- D. Tinted

342 Drinking any amount of alcohol is likely to

Mark three answers
- A. slow down your reactions to hazards
- B. increase the speed of your reactions
- C. worsen your judgement of speed
- D. improve your awareness of danger
- E. give a false sense of confidence

343 What else can seriously affect your concentration, other than alcoholic drinks?

Mark three answers
- A. Drugs
- B. Tiredness
- C. Tinted windows
- D. Contact lenses
- E. Loud music

344 As a driver you find that your eyesight has become very poor. Your optician says they cannot help you. The law says that you should tell

Mark one answer
- A. the licensing authority
- B. your own doctor
- C. the local police station
- D. another optician

345 For which of these may you use hazard warning lights?

Mark one answer

- [ ] **A.** When driving on a motorway to warn traffic behind of a hazard ahead
- [ ] **B.** When you are double parked on a two-way road
- [ ] **C.** When your direction indicators are not working
- [ ] **D.** When warning oncoming traffic that you intend to stop

346 When should you use hazard warning lights?

Mark one answer

- [ ] **A.** When you are double parked on a two-way road
- [ ] **B.** When your direction indicators are not working
- [ ] **C.** When warning oncoming traffic that you intend to stop
- [ ] **D.** When your vehicle has broken down and is causing an obstruction

347 You want to turn left at this junction. The view of the main road is restricted. What should you do?

Mark one answer

- [ ] **A.** Stay well back and wait to see if something comes
- [ ] **B.** Build up your speed so that you can emerge quickly
- [ ] **C.** Stop and apply the handbrake even if the road is clear
- [ ] **D.** Approach slowly and edge out until you can see more clearly

348 You are driving on a motorway. The traffic ahead is braking sharply because of an incident. How could you warn traffic behind you?

Mark one answer

- [ ] **A.** Briefly use the hazard warning lights
- [ ] **B.** Switch on the hazard warning lights continuously
- [ ] **C.** Briefly use the rear fog lights
- [ ] **D.** Switch on the headlights continuously

349 When may you use hazard warning lights?

Mark one answer

- A. To park alongside another car
- B. To park on double yellow lines
- C. When you are being towed
- D. When you have broken down

350 Hazard warning lights should be used when vehicles are

Mark one answer

- A. broken down and causing an obstruction
- B. faulty and moving slowly
- C. being towed along a road
- D. reversing into a side road

351 Some two-way roads are divided into three lanes. Why are these particularly dangerous?

Mark one answer

- A. Traffic in both directions can use the middle lane to overtake
- B. Traffic can travel faster in poor weather conditions
- C. Traffic can overtake on the left
- D. Traffic uses the middle lane for emergencies only

352 When driving a car fitted with automatic transmission what would you use 'kick down' for?

Mark one answer

- A. Cruise control
- B. Quick acceleration
- C. Slow braking
- D. Fuel economy

353 You are waiting to emerge at a junction. Your view is restricted by parked vehicles. What can help you to see traffic on the road you are joining?

Mark one answer

- A. Looking for traffic behind you
- B. Reflections of traffic in shop windows
- C. Making eye contact with other road users
- D. Checking for traffic in your interior mirror

354 Overtaking is a major cause of collisions. In which THREE of these situations should you NOT overtake?

Mark three answers

- A. If you are turning left shortly afterwards
- B. When you are in a one-way street
- C. When you are approaching a junction
- D. If you are travelling up a long hill
- E. When your view ahead is blocked

355 Which sign means that there may be people walking along the road?

Mark one answer

A.

B.

C.

D.

356 You are turning left at a junction. Pedestrians have started to cross the road. You should

Mark one answer
- A. go on, giving them plenty of room
- B. stop and wave at them to cross
- C. blow your horn and proceed
- D. give way to them

357 You are turning left from a main road into a side road. People are already crossing the road into which you are turning. You should

Mark one answer
- A. continue, as it is your right of way
- B. signal to them to continue crossing
- C. wait and allow them to cross
- D. sound your horn to warn them of your presence

358 You are at a road junction, turning into a minor road. There are pedestrians crossing the minor road. You should

Mark one answer
- A. stop and wave the pedestrians across
- B. sound your horn to let the pedestrians know that you are there
- C. give way to the pedestrians who are already crossing
- D. carry on; the pedestrians should give way to you

359 You are turning left into a side road. What hazards should you be especially aware of?

Mark one answer
- A. One-way street
- B. Pedestrians
- C. Traffic congestion
- D. Parked vehicles

360 You intend to turn right into a side road. Just before turning you should check for motorcyclists who might be

Mark one answer
- A. overtaking on your left
- B. following you closely
- C. emerging from the side road
- D. overtaking on your right

361 A toucan crossing is different from other crossings because

Mark one answer
- A. moped riders can use it
- B. it is controlled by a traffic warden
- C. it is controlled by two flashing lights
- D. cyclists can use it

362 At toucan crossings

Mark one answer
- A. you only stop if someone is waiting to cross
- B. cyclists are not permitted
- C. there is a continuously flashing amber beacon
- D. pedestrians and cyclists may cross

363 What does this sign tell you?

Mark one answer
- A. No cycling
- B. Cycle route ahead
- C. Cycle parking only
- D. End of cycle route

364 How will a school crossing patrol signal you to stop?

Mark one answer
- A. By pointing to children on the opposite pavement
- B. By displaying a red light
- C. By displaying a stop sign
- D. By giving you an arm signal

365 Where would you see this sign?

Mark one answer
- A. In the window of a car taking children to school
- B. At the side of the road
- C. At playground areas
- D. On the rear of a school bus or coach

366 Which sign tells you that pedestrians may be walking in the road as there is no pavement?

Mark one answer

A.

B.

C.

D.

367 What does this sign mean?

Mark one answer

A. No route for pedestrians and cyclists
B. A route for pedestrians only
C. A route for cyclists only
D. A route for pedestrians and cyclists

368 You see a pedestrian with a white stick and red band. This means that the person is

Mark one answer

A. physically disabled
B. deaf only
C. blind only
D. deaf and blind

369 What action would you take when elderly people are crossing the road?

Mark one answer

A. Wave them across so they know that you have seen them
B. Be patient and allow them to cross in their own time
C. Rev the engine to let them know that you are waiting
D. Tap the horn in case they are hard of hearing

370 You see two elderly pedestrians about to cross the road ahead. You should

Mark one answer

A. expect them to wait for you to pass
B. speed up to get past them quickly
C. stop and wave them across the road
D. be careful, they may misjudge your speed

371 What does this sign mean?

Mark one answer

A. Contraflow pedal cycle lane
B. With-flow pedal cycle lane
C. Pedal cycles and buses only
D. No pedal cycles or buses

372
You are coming up to a roundabout. A cyclist is signalling to turn right. What should you do?

Mark one answer
- **A.** Overtake on the right
- **B.** Give a horn warning
- **C.** Signal the cyclist to move across
- **D.** Give the cyclist plenty of room

373
You are approaching this roundabout and see the cyclist signal right. Why is the cyclist keeping to the left?

Mark one answer
- **A.** It is a quicker route for the cyclist
- **B.** The cyclist is going to turn left instead
- **C.** The cyclist thinks *The Highway Code* does not apply to bicycles
- **D.** The cyclist is slower and more vulnerable

374
When you are overtaking a cyclist you should leave as much room as you would give to a car. What is the main reason for this?

Mark one answer
- **A.** The cyclist might speed up
- **B.** The cyclist might get off the bike
- **C.** The cyclist might swerve
- **D.** The cyclist might have to make a left turn

375
Which TWO should you allow extra room when overtaking?

Mark two answers
- **A.** Motorcycles
- **B.** Tractors
- **C.** Bicycles
- **D.** Road-sweeping vehicles

376
Why should you look particularly for motorcyclists and cyclists at junctions?

Mark one answer
- **A.** They may want to turn into the side road
- **B.** They may slow down to let you turn
- **C.** They are harder to see
- **D.** They might not see you turn

377
You are waiting to come out of a side road. Why should you watch carefully for motorcycles?

Mark one answer
- **A.** Motorcycles are usually faster than cars
- **B.** Police patrols often use motorcycles
- **C.** Motorcycles are small and hard to see
- **D.** Motorcycles have right of way

378
In daylight, an approaching motorcyclist is using a dipped headlight. Why?

Mark one answer
- **A.** So that the rider can be seen more easily
- **B.** To stop the battery overcharging
- **C.** To improve the rider's vision
- **D.** The rider is inviting you to proceed

379 Motorcyclists should wear bright clothing mainly because

Mark one answer
- A. they must do so by law
- B. it helps keep them cool in summer
- C. the colours are popular
- D. drivers often do not see them

380 There is a slow-moving motorcyclist ahead of you. You are unsure what the rider is going to do. You should

Mark one answer
- A. pass on the left
- B. pass on the right
- C. stay behind
- D. move closer

381 Motorcyclists will often look round over their right shoulder just before turning right. This is because

Mark one answer
- A. they need to listen for following traffic
- B. motorcycles do not have mirrors
- C. looking around helps them balance as they turn
- D. they need to check for traffic in their blind area

382 At road junctions which of the following are most vulnerable?

Mark three answers
- A. Cyclists
- B. Motorcyclists
- C. Pedestrians
- D. Car drivers
- E. Lorry drivers

383 Motorcyclists are particularly vulnerable

Mark one answer
- A. when moving off
- B. on dual carriageways
- C. when approaching junctions
- D. on motorways

384 You notice horse riders in front. What should you do FIRST?

Mark one answer
- A. Pull out to the middle of the road
- B. Slow down and be ready to stop
- C. Accelerate around them
- D. Signal right

385 You are approaching a roundabout. There are horses just ahead of you. You should

Mark two answers

- A. be prepared to stop
- B. treat them like any other vehicle
- C. give them plenty of room
- D. accelerate past as quickly as possible
- E. sound your horn as a warning

386 Which THREE should you do when passing sheep on a road?

Mark three answers

- A. Allow plenty of room
- B. Go very slowly
- C. Pass quickly but quietly
- D. Be ready to stop
- E. Briefly sound your horn

387 At night you see a pedestrian wearing reflective clothing and carrying a bright red light. What does this mean?

Mark one answer

- A. You are approaching road works
- B. You are approaching an organised walk
- C. You are approaching a slow-moving vehicle
- D. You are approaching a traffic danger spot

388 As you approach a pelican crossing the lights change to green. Elderly people are half-way across. You should

Mark one answer

- A. wave them to cross as quickly as they can
- B. rev your engine to make them hurry
- C. flash your lights in case they have not heard you
- D. wait because they will take longer to cross

389 There are flashing amber lights under a school warning sign. What action should you take?

Mark one answer

- A. Reduce speed until you are clear of the area
- B. Keep up your speed and sound the horn
- C. Increase your speed to clear the area quickly
- D. Wait at the lights until they change to green

390 You are approaching this crossing. You should

Mark one answer

- A. prepare to slow down and stop
- B. stop and wave the pedestrians across
- C. speed up and pass by quickly
- D. continue unless the pedestrians step out

391 You see a pedestrian with a dog. The dog has a yellow or burgundy coat. This especially warns you that the pedestrian is

Mark one answer

- A. elderly
- B. dog training
- C. colour blind
- D. deaf

392 These road markings must be kept clear to allow

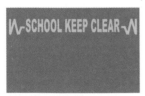

Mark one answer

- A. schoolchildren to be dropped off
- B. for teachers to park
- C. schoolchildren to be picked up
- D. a clear view of the crossing area

393 You must not stop on these road markings because you may obstruct

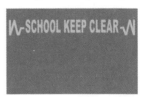

Mark one answer

- A. children's view of the crossing area
- B. teachers' access to the school
- C. delivery vehicles' access to the school
- D. emergency vehicles' access to the school

394 The left-hand pavement is closed due to street repairs. What should you do?

Mark one answer

- A. Watch out for pedestrians walking in the road
- B. Use your right-hand mirror more often
- C. Speed up to get past the road works quicker
- D. Position close to the left-hand kerb

395 Where would you see this sign?

Mark one answer

- A. Near a school crossing
- B. At a playground entrance
- C. On a school bus
- D. At a 'pedestrians only' area

396 You are following a motorcyclist on an uneven road. You should

Mark one answer

- [ ] A. allow less room so you can be seen in their mirrors
- [ ] B. overtake immediately
- [ ] C. allow extra room in case they swerve to avoid potholes
- [ ] D. allow the same room as normal because road surfaces do not affect motorcyclists

397 You are following two cyclists. They approach a roundabout in the left-hand lane. In which direction should you expect the cyclists to go?

Mark one answer

- [ ] A. Left
- [ ] B. Right
- [ ] C. Any direction
- [ ] D. Straight ahead

398 You are travelling behind a moped. You want to turn left just ahead. You should

Mark one answer

- [ ] A. overtake the moped before the junction
- [ ] B. pull alongside the moped and stay level until just before the junction
- [ ] C. sound your horn as a warning and pull in front of the moped
- [ ] D. stay behind until the moped has passed the junction

399 You see a horse rider as you approach a roundabout. They are signalling right but keeping well to the left. You should

Mark one answer

- [ ] A. proceed as normal
- [ ] B. keep close to them
- [ ] C. cut in front of them
- [ ] D. stay well back

400 How would you react to drivers who appear to be inexperienced?

Mark one answer

- [ ] A. Sound your horn to warn them of your presence
- [ ] B. Be patient and prepare for them to react more slowly
- [ ] C. Flash your headlights to indicate that it is safe for them to proceed
- [ ] D. Overtake them as soon as possible

401 You are following a learner driver who stalls at a junction. You should

Mark one answer

- A. be patient as you expect them to make mistakes
- B. stay very close behind and flash your headlights
- C. start to rev your engine if they take too long to restart
- D. immediately steer around them and drive on

402 You are on a country road. What should you expect to see coming towards you on YOUR side of the road?

Mark one answer

- A. Motorcycles
- B. Bicycles
- C. Pedestrians
- D. Horse riders

403 You are turning left into a side road. Pedestrians are crossing the road near the junction. You must

Mark one answer

- A. wave them on
- B. sound your horn
- C. switch on your hazard lights
- D. wait for them to cross

404 You are following a car driven by an elderly driver. You should

Mark one answer

- A. expect the driver to drive badly
- B. flash your lights and overtake
- C. be aware that the driver's reactions may not be as fast as yours
- D. stay very close behind but be careful

405 You are following a cyclist. You wish to turn left just ahead. You should

Mark one answer

- A. overtake the cyclist before the junction
- B. pull alongside the cyclist and stay level until after the junction
- C. hold back until the cyclist has passed the junction
- D. go around the cyclist on the junction

406 A horse rider is in the left-hand lane approaching a roundabout. You should expect the rider to

Mark one answer

- A. go in any direction
- B. turn right
- C. turn left
- D. go ahead

407 You have just passed your test. How can you reduce your risk of a collision?

Mark one answer

- [ ] A. By always staying close to the vehicle in front
- [ ] B. By never going over 40mph
- [ ] C. By staying only in the left-hand lane on all roads
- [ ] D. By taking further training

408 Powered vehicles used by disabled people are small and hard to see. How do they give early warning when on a dual carriageway?

Mark one answer

- [ ] A. They will have a flashing red light
- [ ] B. They will have a flashing green light
- [ ] C. They will have a flashing blue light
- [ ] D. They will have a flashing amber light

409 You should never attempt to overtake a cyclist

Mark one answer

- [ ] A. just before you turn left
- [ ] B. on a left-hand bend
- [ ] C. on a one-way street
- [ ] D. on a dual carriageway

410 Ahead of you there is a moving vehicle with a flashing amber beacon. This means it is

Mark one answer

- [ ] A. slow moving
- [ ] B. broken down
- [ ] C. a doctor's car
- [ ] D. a school crossing patrol

411 You want to reverse into a side road. You are not sure that the area behind your car is clear. What should you do?

Mark one answer

- [ ] A. Look through the rear window only
- [ ] B. Get out and check
- [ ] C. Check the mirrors only
- [ ] D. Carry on, assuming it is clear

412 You are about to reverse into a side road. A pedestrian wishes to cross behind you. You should

Mark one answer

- [ ] A. wave to the pedestrian to stop
- [ ] B. give way to the pedestrian
- [ ] C. wave to the pedestrian to cross
- [ ] D. reverse before the pedestrian starts to cross

413 Who is especially in danger of not being seen as you reverse your car?

Mark one answer

- [ ] A. Motorcyclists
- [ ] B. Car drivers
- [ ] C. Cyclists
- [ ] D. Children

414 You are reversing around a corner when you notice a pedestrian walking behind you. What should you do?

Mark one answer

- [ ] A. Slow down and wave the pedestrian across
- [ ] B. Continue reversing and steer round the pedestrian
- [ ] C. Stop and give way
- [ ] D. Continue reversing and sound your horn

415 You want to turn right from a junction but your view is restricted by parked vehicles. What should you do?

Mark one answer

- [ ] A. Move out quickly, but be prepared to stop
- [ ] B. Sound your horn and pull out if there is no reply
- [ ] C. Stop, then move slowly forward until you have a clear view
- [ ] D. Stop, get out and look along the main road to check

416 You are at the front of a queue of traffic waiting to turn right into a side road. Why is it important to check your right mirror just before turning?

Mark one answer

- [ ] A. To look for pedestrians about to cross
- [ ] B. To check for overtaking vehicles
- [ ] C. To make sure the side road is clear
- [ ] D. To check for emerging traffic

417 What must a driver do at a pelican crossing when the amber light is flashing?

Mark one answer

- [ ] A. Signal the pedestrian to cross
- [ ] B. Always wait for the green light before proceeding
- [ ] C. Give way to any pedestrians on the crossing
- [ ] D. Wait for the red-and-amber light before proceeding

418 You have stopped at a pelican crossing. A disabled person is crossing slowly in front of you. The lights have now changed to green. You should

Mark two answers

- [ ] A. allow the person to cross
- [ ] B. drive in front of the person
- [ ] C. drive behind the person
- [ ] D. sound your horn
- [ ] E. be patient
- [ ] F. edge forward slowly

419 You are driving past parked cars. You notice a bicycle wheel sticking out between them. What should you do?

Mark one answer

- [ ] A. Accelerate past quickly and sound your horn
- [ ] B. Slow down and wave the cyclist across
- [ ] C. Brake sharply and flash your headlights
- [ ] D. Slow down and be prepared to stop for a cyclist

420 You are driving past a line of parked cars. You notice a ball bouncing out into the road ahead. What should you do?

Mark one answer

- [ ] **A.** Continue driving at the same speed and sound your horn
- [ ] **B.** Continue driving at the same speed and flash your headlights
- [ ] **C.** Slow down and be prepared to stop for children
- [ ] **D.** Stop and wave the children across to fetch their ball

421 You want to turn right from a main road into a side road. Just before turning you should

Mark one answer

- [ ] **A.** cancel your right-turn signal
- [ ] **B.** select first gear
- [ ] **C.** check for traffic overtaking on your right
- [ ] **D.** stop and set the handbrake

422 You are driving in slow-moving queues of traffic. Just before changing lane you should

Mark one answer

- [ ] **A.** sound the horn
- [ ] **B.** look for motorcyclists filtering through the traffic
- [ ] **C.** give a 'slowing down' arm signal
- [ ] **D.** change down to first gear

423 You are driving in town. There is a bus at the bus stop on the other side of the road. Why should you be careful?

Mark one answer

- [ ] **A.** The bus may have broken down
- [ ] **B.** Pedestrians may come from behind the bus
- [ ] **C.** The bus may move off suddenly
- [ ] **D.** The bus may remain stationary

424 How should you overtake horse riders?

Mark one answer

- [ ] **A.** Drive up close and overtake as soon as possible
- [ ] **B.** Speed is not important but allow plenty of room
- [ ] **C.** Use your horn just once to warn them
- [ ] **D.** Drive slowly and leave plenty of room

425 You are dazzled at night by a vehicle behind you. You should

Mark one answer

- [ ] **A.** set your mirror to anti-dazzle
- [ ] **B.** set your mirror to dazzle the other driver
- [ ] **C.** brake sharply to a stop
- [ ] **D.** switch your rear lights on and off

426 Yellow zigzag lines on the road outside schools mean

Mark one answer

- [ ] **A.** sound your horn to alert other road users
- [ ] **B.** stop to allow children to cross
- [ ] **C.** you must not park or stop on these lines
- [ ] **D.** you must not drive over these lines

427 What do these road markings outside a school mean?

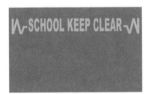

Mark one answer

- [ ] **A.** You may park here if you are a teacher
- [ ] **B.** Sound your horn before parking
- [ ] **C.** When parking, use your hazard warning lights
- [ ] **D.** You should not wait or park your vehicle here

428 You are driving on a main road. You intend to turn right into a side road. Just before turning you should

Mark one answer

- [ ] **A.** adjust your interior mirror
- [ ] **B.** flash your headlamps
- [ ] **C.** steer over to the left
- [ ] **D.** check for traffic overtaking on your right

429 Why should you allow extra room when overtaking a motorcyclist on a windy day?

Mark one answer

- [ ] **A.** The rider may turn off suddenly to get out of the wind
- [ ] **B.** The rider may be blown across in front of you
- [ ] **C.** The rider may stop suddenly
- [ ] **D.** The rider may be travelling faster than normal

430 You are driving towards a zebra crossing. A person in a wheelchair is waiting to cross. What should you do?

Mark one answer

- [ ] **A.** Continue on your way
- [ ] **B.** Wave to the person to cross
- [ ] **C.** Wave to the person to wait
- [ ] **D.** Be prepared to stop

431 Where in particular should you look out for motorcyclists?

Mark one answer

- **A.** In a filling station
- **B.** At a road junction
- **C.** Near a service area
- **D.** When entering a car park

432 Where should you take particular care to look out for motorcyclists and cyclists?

Mark one answer

- **A.** On dual carriageways
- **B.** At junctions
- **C.** At zebra crossings
- **D.** On one-way streets

433 The road outside this school is marked with yellow zigzag lines. What do these lines mean?

Mark one answer

- **A.** You may park on the lines when dropping off schoolchildren
- **B.** You may park on the lines when picking schoolchildren up
- **C.** You must not wait or park your vehicle here at all
- **D.** You must stay with your vehicle if you park here

434 Some junctions controlled by traffic lights have a marked area between two stop lines. What is this for?

Mark one answer

- **A.** To allow taxis to position in front of other traffic
- **B.** To allow people with disabilities to cross the road
- **C.** To allow cyclists and pedestrians to cross the road together
- **D.** To allow cyclists to position in front of other traffic

435 At some traffic lights there are advance stop lines and a marked area. What are these for?

Mark one answer

- **A.** To allow cyclists to position in front of other traffic
- **B.** To let pedestrians cross when the lights change
- **C.** To prevent traffic from jumping the lights
- **D.** To let passengers get off a bus which is queuing

436 You are about to overtake a slow-moving motorcyclist. Which one of these signs would make you take special care?

Mark one answer

A.

B.

C.

D.

437 You are waiting to emerge left from a minor road. A large vehicle is approaching from the right. You have time to turn, but you should wait. Why?

Mark one answer

A. The large vehicle can easily hide an overtaking vehicle
B. The large vehicle can turn suddenly
C. The large vehicle is difficult to steer in a straight line
D. The large vehicle can easily hide vehicles from the left

438 You are following a long vehicle. It approaches a crossroads and signals left, but moves out to the right. You should

Mark one answer

A. get closer in order to pass it quickly
B. stay well back and give it room
C. assume the signal is wrong and It Is really turning right
D. overtake as it starts to slow down

439 You are following a long vehicle approaching a crossroads. The driver signals right but moves close to the left-hand kerb. What should you do?

Mark one answer

A. Warn the driver of the wrong signal
B. Wait behind the long vehicle
C. Report the driver to the police
D. Overtake on the right-hand side

440

You are approaching a mini-roundabout. The long vehicle in front is signalling left but positioned over to the right. You should

Mark one answer

- **A.** sound your horn
- **B.** overtake on the left
- **C.** follow the same course as the lorry
- **D.** keep well back

441

Before overtaking a large vehicle you should keep well back. Why is this?

Mark one answer

- **A.** To give acceleration space to overtake quickly on blind bends
- **B.** To get the best view of the road ahead
- **C.** To leave a gap in case the vehicle stops and rolls back
- **D.** To offer other drivers a safe gap if they want to overtake you

442

Why is it more difficult to overtake a large vehicle than a car?

Mark one answer

- **A.** It takes longer to pass one
- **B.** They may suddenly pull up
- **C.** Their brakes are not as good
- **D.** They climb hills more slowly

443

You are travelling behind a bus that pulls up at a bus stop. What should you do?

Mark two answers

- **A.** Accelerate past the bus sounding your horn
- **B.** Watch carefully for pedestrians
- **C.** Be ready to give way to the bus
- **D.** Pull in closely behind the bus

444

When you approach a bus signalling to move off from a bus stop you should

Mark one answer

- **A.** get past before it moves
- **B.** allow it to pull away, if it is safe to do so
- **C.** flash your headlights as you approach
- **D.** signal left and wave the bus on

445 Which of these is LEAST likely to be affected by crosswinds?

Mark one answer

A. Cyclists
B. Motorcyclists
C. High-sided vehicles
D. Cars

446 You are following a large lorry on a wet road. Spray makes it difficult to see. You should

Mark one answer

A. drop back until you can see better
B. put your headlights on full beam
C. keep close to the lorry, away from the spray
D. speed up and overtake quickly

447 What should you do as you approach this lorry?

Mark one answer

A. Slow down and be prepared to wait
B. Make the lorry wait for you
C. Flash your lights at the lorry
D. Move to the right-hand side of the road

448 You are following a large articulated vehicle. It is going to turn left into a narrow road. What action should you take?

Mark one answer

A. Move out and overtake on the right
B. Pass on the left as the vehicle moves out
C. Be prepared to stop behind
D. Overtake quickly before the lorry moves out

449 You keep well back while waiting to overtake a large vehicle. A car fills the gap. You should

Mark one answer

A. sound your horn
B. drop back further
C. flash your headlights
D. start to overtake

450 You are following a large vehicle approaching crossroads. The driver signals to turn left. What should you do?

Mark one answer

A. Overtake if you can leave plenty of room
B. Overtake only if there are no oncoming vehicles
C. Do not overtake until the vehicle begins to turn
D. Do not overtake when at or approaching a junction

451 You are following a long lorry. The driver signals to turn left into a narrow road. What should you do?

Mark one answer

- [ ] **A.** Overtake on the left before the lorry reaches the junction
- [ ] **B.** Overtake on the right as soon as the lorry slows down
- [ ] **C.** Do not overtake unless you can see there is no oncoming traffic
- [ ] **D.** Do not overtake, stay well back and be prepared to stop

452 You wish to overtake a long, slow-moving vehicle on a busy road. You should

Mark one answer

- [ ] **A.** follow it closely and keep moving out to see the road ahead
- [ ] **B.** flash your headlights for the oncoming traffic to give way
- [ ] **C.** stay behind until the driver waves you past
- [ ] **D.** keep well back until you can see that it is clear

453 It is very windy. You are behind a motorcyclist who is overtaking a high-sided vehicle. What should you do?

Mark one answer

- [ ] **A.** Overtake the motorcyclist immediately
- [ ] **B.** Keep well back
- [ ] **C.** Stay level with the motorcyclist
- [ ] **D.** Keep close to the motorcyclist

454 It is very windy. You are about to overtake a motorcyclist. You should

Mark one answer

- [ ] **A.** overtake slowly
- [ ] **B.** allow extra room
- [ ] **C.** sound your horn
- [ ] **D.** keep close as you pass

455 You are towing a caravan. Which is the safest type of rear-view mirror to use?

Mark one answer

- [ ] **A.** Interior wide-angle mirror
- [ ] **B.** Extended-arm side mirrors
- [ ] **C.** Ordinary door mirrors
- [ ] **D.** Ordinary interior mirror

456 You are driving in town. Ahead of you a bus is at a bus stop. Which TWO of the following should you do?

Mark two answers

- [ ] **A.** Be prepared to give way if the bus suddenly moves off
- [ ] **B.** Continue at the same speed but sound your horn as a warning
- [ ] **C.** Watch carefully for the sudden appearance of pedestrians
- [ ] **D.** Pass the bus as quickly as you possibly can

457 You are driving in heavy traffic on a wet road. Spray makes it difficult to be seen. You should use your

Mark two answers
- [ ] **A.** full beam headlights
- [ ] **B.** rear fog lights if visibility is less than 10ᶜ metres (328 feet)
- [ ] **C.** rear fog lights if visibility is more than 100 metres (328 feet)
- [ ] **D.** dipped headlights
- [ ] **E.** sidelights only

458 You are driving along this road. What should you be prepared to do?

Mark one answer
- [ ] **A.** Sound your horn and continue
- [ ] **B.** Slow down and give way
- [ ] **C.** Report the driver to the police
- [ ] **D.** Squeeze through the gap

459 As a driver why should you be more careful where trams operate?

Mark one answer
- [ ] **A.** Because they do not have a horn
- [ ] **B.** Because they do not stop for cars
- [ ] **C.** Because they do not have lights
- [ ] **D.** Because they cannot steer to avoid you

460 It is a very windy day and you are about to overtake a cyclist. What should you do?

Mark one answer
- [ ] **A.** Overtake very closely
- [ ] **B.** Keep close as you pass
- [ ] **C.** Sound your horn repeatedly
- [ ] **D.** Allow extra room

461 Powered vehicles, such as wheelchairs or scooters, used by disabled people have a maximum speed of

Mark one answer
- [ ] **A.** 8mph
- [ ] **B.** 12mph
- [ ] **C.** 16mph
- [ ] **D.** 20mph

462 In front of you is a Class 3 powered vehicle (powered wheelchair) driven by a disabled person. These vehicles have a maximum speed of

Mark one answer
- [ ] **A.** 8mph (12km/h)
- [ ] **B.** 18mph (29km/h)
- [ ] **C.** 28mph (45km/h)
- [ ] **D.** 38mph (61km/h)

463 In which THREE of these situations may you overtake another vehicle on the left?

Mark three answers

- A. When you are in a one-way street
- B. When approaching a motorway slip road where you will be turning off
- C. When the vehicle in front is signalling to turn right
- D. When a slower vehicle is travelling in the right-hand lane of a dual carriageway
- E. In slow-moving traffic queues when traffic in the right-hand lane is moving more slowly

464 You are travelling in very heavy rain. Your overall stopping distance is likely to be

Mark one answer

- A. doubled
- B. halved
- C. up to ten times greater
- D. no different

465 Which TWO of the following are correct? When overtaking at night you should

Mark two answers

- A. wait until a bend so that you can see the oncoming headlights
- B. sound your horn twice before moving out
- C. be careful because you can see less
- D. beware of bends in the road ahead
- E. put headlights on full beam

466 When may you wait in a box junction?

Mark one answer

- A. When you are stationary in a queue of traffic
- B. When approaching a pelican crossing
- C. When approaching a zebra crossing
- D. When oncoming traffic prevents you turning right

467 Which of these plates normally appear with this road sign?

Mark one answer

- A. Humps for ½ mile
- B. Hump Bridge
- C. Low Bridge
- D. Soft Verge

468 Areas reserved for trams may have

Mark three answers
- A. metal studs around them
- B. white line markings
- C. zigzag markings
- D. a different coloured surface
- E. yellow hatch markings
- F. a different surface texture

469 Traffic calming measures are used to

Mark one answer
- A. stop road rage
- B. help overtaking
- C. slow traffic down
- D. help parking

470 Why should you always reduce your speed when travelling in fog?

Mark one answer
- A. The brakes do not work as well
- B. You will be dazzled by other headlights
- C. The engine will take longer to warm up
- D. It is more difficult to see events ahead

471 You are on a motorway in fog. The left-hand edge of the motorway can be identified by reflective studs. What colour are they?

Mark one answer
- A. Green
- B. Amber
- C. Red
- D. White

472 A rumble device is designed to

Mark two answers
- A. give directions
- B. prevent cattle escaping
- C. alert you to low tyre pressure
- D. alert you to a hazard
- E. encourage you to reduce speed

473 After this hazard you should test your brakes. Why is this?

Ford

Mark one answer
- A. You will be on a slippery road
- B. Your brakes will be soaking wet
- C. You will be going down a long hill
- D. You will have just crossed a long bridge

474 You have to make a journey in foggy conditions. You should

Mark one answer

- [ ] **A.** follow other vehicles' tail-lights closely
- [ ] **B.** avoid using dipped headlights
- [ ] **C.** leave plenty of time for your journey
- [ ] **D.** keep two seconds behind other vehicles

475 You see a vehicle coming towards you on a single-track road. You should

Mark one answer

- [ ] **A.** go back to the main road
- [ ] **B.** do an emergency stop
- [ ] **C.** stop at a passing place
- [ ] **D.** put on your hazard warning lights

476 You are overtaking a car at night. You must be sure that

Mark one answer

- [ ] **A.** you flash your headlights before overtaking
- [ ] **B.** you select a higher gear
- [ ] **C.** you have switched your lights to full beam before overtaking
- [ ] **D.** you do not dazzle other road users

477 You are on a road which has speed humps. A driver in front is travelling slower than you. You should

Mark one answer

- [ ] **A.** sound your horn
- [ ] **B.** overtake as soon as you can
- [ ] **C.** flash your headlights
- [ ] **D.** slow down and stay behind

478 You see these markings on the road. Why are they there?

Mark one answer

- [ ] **A.** To show a safe distance between vehicles
- [ ] **B.** To keep the area clear of traffic
- [ ] **C.** To make you aware of your speed
- [ ] **D.** To warn you to change direction

479 When MUST you use dipped headlights during the day?

Mark one answer

- [ ] **A.** All the time
- [ ] **B.** Along narrow streets
- [ ] **C.** In poor visibility
- [ ] **D.** When parking

480 What are TWO main reasons why coasting downhill is wrong?

Mark two answers

- A. Fuel consumption will be higher
- B. The vehicle will get faster
- C. It puts more wear and tear on the tyres
- D. You have less braking and steering control
- E. It damages the engine

481 Hills can affect the performance of your vehicle. Which TWO apply when driving up steep hills?

Mark two answers

- A. Higher gears will pull better
- B. You will slow down sooner
- C. Overtaking will be easier
- D. The engine will work harder
- E. The steering will feel heavier

482 Why is travelling in neutral for long distances (known as coasting) wrong?

Mark one answer

- A. It will cause the car to skid
- B. It will make the engine stall
- C. The engine will run faster
- D. There is no engine braking

483 You are driving on the motorway in windy conditions. When passing high-sided vehicles you should

Mark one answer

- A. increase your speed
- B. be wary of a sudden gust
- C. drive alongside very closely
- D. expect normal conditions

484 To correct a rear-wheel skid you should

Mark one answer

- A. not steer at all
- B. steer away from it
- C. steer into it
- D. apply your handbrake

485 You have to make a journey in fog. What are the TWO most important things you should do before you set out?

Mark two answers

- A. Top up the radiator with antifreeze
- B. Make sure that you have a warning triangle in the vehicle
- C. Check that your lights are working
- D. Check the battery
- E. Make sure that the windows are clean

486 You are driving in fog. Why should you keep well back from the vehicle in front?

Mark one answer

- A. In case it changes direction suddenly
- B. In case its fog lights dazzle you
- C. In case it stops suddenly
- D. In case its brake lights dazzle you

487 You should switch your rear fog lights on when visibility drops below

Mark one answer

- A. your overall stopping distance
- B. ten car lengths
- C. 200 metres (656 feet)
- D. 100 metres (328 feet)

488 Whilst driving, the fog clears and you can see more clearly. You must remember to

Mark one answer
- A. switch off the fog lights
- B. reduce your speed
- C. switch off the demister
- D. close any open windows

489 You have to park on the road in fog. You should

Mark one answer
- A. leave sidelights on
- B. leave dipped headlights and fog lights on
- C. leave dipped headlights on
- D. leave main beam headlights on

490 On a foggy day you unavoidably have to park your car on the road. You should

Mark one answer
- A. leave your headlights on
- B. leave your fog lights on
- C. leave your sidelights on
- D. leave your hazard lights on

491 You are travelling at night. You are dazzled by headlights coming towards you. You should

Mark one answer
- A. pull down your sun visor
- B. slow down or stop
- C. switch on your main beam headlights
- D. put your hand over your eyes

492 Which FOUR of the following may apply when dealing with this hazard?

Ford

Mark four answers
- A. It could be more difficult in winter
- B. Use a low gear and drive slowly
- C. Use a high gear to prevent wheelspin
- D. Test your brakes afterwards
- E. Always switch on fog lamps
- F. There may be a depth gauge

493 Front fog lights may be used ONLY if

Mark one answer
- A. visibility is seriously reduced
- B. they are fitted above the bumper
- C. they are not as bright as the headlights
- D. an audible warning device is used

494 Front fog lights may be used ONLY if

Mark one answer
- A. your headlights are not working
- B. they are operated with rear fog lights
- C. they were fitted by the vehicle manufacturer
- D. visibility is seriously reduced

495
You are driving with your front fog lights switched on. Earlier fog has now cleared. What should you do?

Mark one answer

- A. Leave them on if other drivers have their lights on
- B. Switch them off as long as visibility remains good
- C. Flash them to warn oncoming traffic that it is foggy
- D. Drive with them on instead of your headlights

496
Front fog lights should be used ONLY when

Mark one answer

- A. travelling in very light rain
- B. visibility is seriously reduced
- C. daylight is fading
- D. driving after midnight

497
Why is it dangerous to leave rear fog lights on when they are not needed?

Mark two answers

- A. Brake lights are less clear
- B. Following drivers can be dazzled
- C. Electrical systems could be overloaded
- D. Direction indicators may not work properly
- E. The battery could fail

498
Using rear fog lights on a clear dry night will

Mark two answers

- A. reduce glare from the road surface
- B. make your brake lights less visible
- C. give a better view of the road ahead
- D. dazzle following drivers
- E. help your indicators to be seen more clearly

499
You have just driven out of fog. Visibility is now good. You MUST

Mark one answer

- A. switch off all your fog lights
- B. keep your rear fog lights on
- C. keep your front fog lights on
- D. leave fog lights on in case fog returns

500
You forget to switch off your rear fog lights when the fog has cleared. This may

Mark three answers

- A. dazzle other road users
- B. reduce battery life
- C. cause brake lights to be less clear
- D. be breaking the law
- E. seriously affect engine power

501
You have been driving in thick fog which has now cleared. You must switch OFF your rear fog lights because

Mark one answer

- A. they use a lot of power from the battery
- B. they make your brake lights less clear
- C. they will cause dazzle in your rear-view mirrors
- D. they may not be properly adjusted

502 Front fog lights should be used

Mark one answer

- [ ] A. when visibility is reduced to 100 metres (328 feet)
- [ ] B. as a warning to oncoming traffic
- [ ] C. when driving during the hours of darkness
- [ ] D. in any conditions and at any time

503 Using rear fog lights in clear daylight will

Mark one answer

- [ ] A. be useful when towing a trailer
- [ ] B. give extra protection
- [ ] C. dazzle other drivers
- [ ] D. make following drivers keep back

504 Using front fog lights in clear daylight will

Mark one answer

- [ ] A. flatten the battery
- [ ] B. dazzle other drivers
- [ ] C. improve your visibility
- [ ] D. increase your awareness

505 You may use front fog lights with headlights ONLY when visibility is reduced to less than

Mark one answer

- [ ] A. 100 metres (328 feet)
- [ ] B. 200 metres (656 feet)
- [ ] C. 300 metres (984 feet)
- [ ] D. 400 metres (1,312 feet)

506 You may drive with front fog lights switched on

Mark one answer

- [ ] A. when visibility is less than 100 metres (328 feet)
- [ ] B. at any time to be noticed
- [ ] C. instead of headlights on high-speed roads
- [ ] D. when dazzled by the lights of oncoming vehicles

507 Chains can be fitted to your wheels to help prevent

Mark one answer

- [ ] A. damage to the road surface
- [ ] B. wear to the tyres
- [ ] C. skidding in deep snow
- [ ] D. the brakes locking

508 Holding the clutch pedal down or rolling in neutral for too long while driving will

Mark one answer

- [ ] A. use more fuel
- [ ] B. cause the engine to overheat
- [ ] C. reduce your control
- [ ] D. improve tyre wear

509 How can you use the engine of your vehicle to control your speed?

Mark one answer
- A. By changing to a lower gear
- B. By selecting reverse gear
- C. By changing to a higher gear
- D. By selecting neutral

510 You are driving down a steep hill. Why could keeping the clutch down or rolling in neutral for too long be dangerous?

Mark one answer
- A. Fuel consumption will be higher
- B. Your vehicle will pick up speed
- C. It will damage the engine
- D. It will wear tyres out more quickly

511 Why could keeping the clutch down or selecting neutral for long periods of time be dangerous?

Mark one answer
- A. Fuel spillage will occur
- B. Engine damage may be caused
- C. You will have less steering and braking control
- D. It will wear tyres out more quickly

512 You are driving on an icy road. What distance should you drive from the car in front?

Mark one answer
- A. four times the normal distance
- B. six times the normal distance
- C. eight times the normal distance
- D. ten times the normal distance

513 You are on a well-lit motorway at night. You must

Mark one answer
- A. use only your sidelights
- B. always use your headlights
- C. always use rear fog lights
- D. use headlights only in bad weather

514 You are on a motorway at night with other vehicles just ahead of you. Which lights should you have on?

Mark one answer
- A. Front fog lights
- B. Main beam headlights
- C. Sidelights only
- D. Dipped headlights

515 Which THREE of the following will affect your stopping distance?

Mark three answers
- A. How fast you are going
- B. The tyres on your vehicle
- C. The time of day
- D. The weather
- E. The street lighting

516 You are on a motorway at night. You MUST have your headlights switched on unless

Mark one answer
- A. there are vehicles close in front of you
- B. you are travelling below 50mph
- C. the motorway is lit
- D. your vehicle is broken down on the hard shoulder

517 You will feel the effects of engine braking when you

Mark one answer
- [ ] A. only use the handbrake
- [ ] B. only use neutral
- [ ] C. change to a lower gear
- [ ] D. change to a higher gear

518 Daytime visibility is poor but not seriously reduced. You should switch on

Mark one answer
- [ ] A. headlights and fog lights
- [ ] B. front fog lights
- [ ] C. dipped headlights
- [ ] D. rear fog lights

519 Why are vehicles fitted with rear fog lights?

Mark one answer
- [ ] A. To be seen when driving at high speed
- [ ] B. To use if broken down in a dangerous position
- [ ] C. To make them more visible in thick fog
- [ ] D. To warn drivers following closely to drop back

520 While you are driving in fog, it becomes necessary to use front fog lights. You should

Mark one answer
- [ ] A. only turn them on in heavy traffic conditions
- [ ] B. remember not to use them on motorways
- [ ] C. only use them on dual carriageways
- [ ] D. remember to switch them off as visibility improves

521 When snow is falling heavily you should

Mark one answer
- [ ] A. only drive with your hazard lights on
- [ ] B. not drive unless you have a mobile phone
- [ ] C. only drive when your journey is short
- [ ] D. not drive unless it is essential

522 You are driving down a long steep hill. You suddenly notice your brakes are not working as well as normal. What is the usual cause of this?

Mark one answer
- [ ] A. The brakes overheating
- [ ] B. Air in the brake fluid
- [ ] C. Oil on the brakes
- [ ] D. Badly adjusted brakes

523 The road is wet. Why might a motorcyclist steer round drain covers on a bend?

Mark one answer
- [ ] A. To avoid puncturing the tyres on the edge of the drain covers
- [ ] B. To prevent the motorcycle sliding on the metal drain covers
- [ ] C. To help judge the bend using the drain covers as marker points
- [ ] D. To avoid splashing pedestrians on the pavement

524 You are braking on a wet road. Your vehicle begins to skid. It does not have anti-lock brakes. What is the FIRST thing you should do?

Mark one answer
- [ ] A. Quickly pull up the handbrake
- [ ] B. Release the footbrake
- [ ] C. Push harder on the brake pedal
- [ ] D. Gently use the accelerator

525 Which FOUR of these must NOT use motorways?

Mark four answers
- A. Learner car drivers
- B. Motorcycles over 50cc
- C. Double-deck buses
- D. Farm tractors
- E. Horse riders
- F. Cyclists

526 Which FOUR of these must NOT use motorways?

Mark four answers
- A. Learner car drivers
- B. Motorcycles over 50cc
- C. Double-deck buses
- D. Farm tractors
- E. Learner motorcyclists
- F. Cyclists

527 Immediately after joining a motorway you should normally

Mark one answer
- A. try to overtake
- B. re-adjust your mirrors
- C. position your vehicle in the centre lane
- D. keep in the left-hand lane

528 When joining a motorway you must always

Mark one answer
- A. use the hard shoulder
- B. stop at the end of the acceleration lane
- C. come to a stop before joining the motorway
- D. give way to traffic already on the motorway

529 What is the national speed limit for cars and motorcycles in the centre lane of a three-lane motorway?

Mark one answer
- A. 40mph
- B. 50mph
- C. 60mph
- D. 70mph

530 What is the national speed limit on motorways for cars and motorcycles?

Mark one answer
- A. 30mph
- B. 50mph
- C. 60mph
- D. 70mph

531 The left-hand lane on a three-lane motorway is for use by

Mark one answer
- A. any vehicle
- B. large vehicles only
- C. emergency vehicles only
- D. slow vehicles only

532 What is the right-hand lane used for on a three-lane motorway?

Mark one answer
- A. Emergency vehicles only
- B. Overtaking
- C. Vehicles towing trailers
- D. Coaches only

533
Which of these IS NOT allowed to travel in the right-hand lane of a three-lane motorway?

Mark one answer
- A. A small delivery van
- B. A motorcycle
- C. A vehicle towing a trailer
- D. A motorcycle and sidecar

534
You are on a motorway. You become tired and decide you need to rest. What should you do?

Mark one answer
- A. Stop on the hard shoulder
- B. Pull up on a slip road
- C. Park on the central reservation
- D. Leave at the next exit

535
You break down on a motorway. You need to call for help. Why may it be better to use an emergency roadside telephone rather than a mobile phone?

Mark one answer
- A. It connects you to a local garage
- B. Using a mobile phone will distract other drivers
- C. It allows easy location by the emergency services
- D. Mobile phones do not work on motorways

536
What should you use the hard shoulder of a motorway for?

Mark one answer
- A. Stopping in an emergency
- B. Leaving the motorway
- C. Stopping when you are tired
- D. Joining the motorway

537
After a breakdown you need to rejoin the main carriageway of a motorway from the hard shoulder. You should

Mark one answer
- A. move out onto the carriageway then build up your speed
- B. move out onto the carriageway using your hazard lights
- C. gain speed on the hard shoulder before moving out onto the carriageway
- D. wait on the hard shoulder until someone flashes their headlights at you

538
A crawler lane on a motorway is found

Mark one answer
- A. on a steep gradient
- B. before a service area
- C. before a junction
- D. along the hard shoulder

539 You are on a motorway. There are red flashing lights above every lane. You must

Mark one answer

- A. pull on to the hard shoulder
- B. slow down and watch for further signals
- C. leave at the next exit
- D. stop and wait

540 You are in the right-hand lane on a motorway. You see these overhead signs. This means

Mark one answer

- A. move to the left and reduce your speed to 50mph
- B. there are road works 50 metres (55 yards) ahead
- C. use the hard shoulder until you have passed the hazard
- D. leave the motorway at the next exit

541 What do these motorway signs show?

Mark one answer

- A. They are countdown markers to a bridge
- B. They are distance markers to the next telephone
- C. They are countdown markers to the next exit
- D. They warn of a police control ahead

542 On a motorway the amber reflective studs can be found between

Mark one answer

- A. the hard shoulder and the carriageway
- B. the acceleration lane and the carriageway
- C. the central reservation and the carriageway
- D. each pair of the lanes

543 What colour are the reflective studs between the lanes on a motorway?

Mark one answer

- A. Green
- B. Amber
- C. White
- D. Red

544 What colour are the reflective studs between a motorway and its slip road?

Mark one answer

- A. Amber
- B. White
- C. Green
- D. Red

545 You are allowed to stop on a motorway when you

Mark one answer

- A. need to walk and get fresh air
- B. wish to pick up hitchhikers
- C. are told to do so by flashing red lights
- D. need to use a mobile telephone

546 You have broken down on a motorway. To find the nearest emergency telephone you should always walk

Mark one answer

- A. with the traffic flow
- B. facing oncoming traffic
- C. in the direction shown on the marker posts
- D. in the direction of the nearest exit

547 You are travelling along the left-hand lane of a three-lane motorway. Traffic is joining from a slip road. You should

Mark one answer

- A. race the other vehicles
- B. move to another lane
- C. maintain a steady speed
- D. switch on your hazard flashers

548 You are joining a motorway. Why is it important to make full use of the slip road?

Mark one answer

- A. Because there is space available to turn round if you need to
- B. To allow you direct access to the overtaking lanes
- C. To build up a speed similar to traffic on the motorway
- D. Because you can continue on the hard shoulder

549 How should you use the emergency telephone on a motorway?

Mark one answer

- A. Stay close to the carriageway
- B. Face the oncoming traffic
- C. Keep your back to the traffic
- D. Stand on the hard shoulder

550 You are on a motorway. What colour are the reflective studs on the left of the carriageway?

Mark one answer

- A. Green
- B. Red
- C. White
- D. Amber

551 On a three-lane motorway which lane should you normally use?

Mark one answer

- A. Left
- B. Right
- C. Centre
- D. Either the right or centre

552 A basic rule when on motorways is

Mark one answer

- A. use the lane that has least traffic
- B. keep to the left-hand lane unless overtaking
- C. overtake on the side that is clearest
- D. try to keep above 50mph to prevent congestion

553 When going through a contraflow system on a motorway you should

Mark one answer
- A. ensure that you do not exceed 30mph
- B. keep a good distance from the vehicle ahead
- C. switch lanes to keep the traffic flowing
- D. stay close to the vehicle ahead to reduce queues

554 You are on a three-lane motorway. There are red reflective studs on your left and white ones to your right. Where are you?

Mark one answer
- A. In the right-hand lane
- B. In the middle lane
- C. On the hard shoulder
- D. In the left-hand lane

555 When should you stop on a motorway?

Mark three answers
- A. If you have to read a map
- B. When you are tired and need a rest
- C. If red lights show above every lane
- D. When told to by the police
- E. If your mobile phone rings
- F. When signalled by a Highways Agency Traffic Officer

556 You are approaching road works on a motorway. What should you do?

Mark one answer
- A. Speed up to clear the area quickly
- B. Always use the hard shoulder
- C. Obey all speed limits
- D. Stay very close to the vehicle in front

557 On motorways you should never overtake on the left unless

Mark one answer
- A. you can see well ahead that the hard shoulder is clear
- B. the traffic in the right-hand lane is signalling right
- C. you warn drivers behind by signalling left
- D. there is a queue of slow-moving traffic to your right that is moving more slowly than you are

558 You are towing a trailer on a motorway. What is your maximum speed limit?

Mark one answer
- [ ] A. 40mph
- [ ] B. 50mph
- [ ] C. 60mph
- [ ] D. 70mph

559 The left-hand lane of a motorway should be used for

Mark one answer
- [ ] A. breakdowns and emergencies only
- [ ] B. overtaking slower traffic in the other lanes
- [ ] C. slow vehicles only
- [ ] D. normal driving

560 You are driving on a motorway. You have to slow down quickly due to a hazard. You should

Mark one answer
- [ ] A. switch on your hazard lights
- [ ] B. switch on your headlights
- [ ] C. sound your horn
- [ ] D. flash your headlights

561 You get a puncture on the motorway. You manage to get your vehicle onto the hard shoulder. You should

Mark one answer
- [ ] A. change the wheel yourself immediately
- [ ] B. use the emergency telephone and call for assistance
- [ ] C. try to wave down another vehicle for help
- [ ] D. only change the wheel if you have a passenger to help you

562 You are driving on a motorway. By mistake, you go past the exit that you wanted to take. You should

Mark one answer
- [ ] A. carefully reverse on the hard shoulder
- [ ] B. carry on to the next exit
- [ ] C. carefully reverse in the left-hand lane
- [ ] D. make a U-turn at the next gap in the central reservation

563 Your vehicle breaks down on the hard shoulder of a motorway. You decide to use your mobile phone to call for help. You should

Mark one answer
- [ ] A. stand at the rear of the vehicle while making the call
- [ ] B. try to repair the vehicle yourself
- [ ] C. get out of the vehicle by the right-hand door
- [ ] D. check your location from the marker posts on the left

564 You are travelling on a motorway. Unless signs show a lower speed limit you must NOT exceed

NI

Mark one answer
- [ ] A. 50mph
- [ ] B. 60mph
- [ ] C. 70mph
- [ ] D. 80mph

565 You are on a three-lane motorway towing a trailer. You may use the right-hand lane when

NI

Mark one answer
- [ ] A. there are lane closures
- [ ] B. there is slow-moving traffic
- [ ] C. you can maintain a high speed
- [ ] D. large vehicles are in the left and centre lanes

566
You are on a motorway. There is a contraflow system ahead. What would you expect to find?

Mark one answer

- A. Temporary traffic lights
- B. Lower speed limits
- C. Wider lanes than normal
- D. Speed humps

567
You are driving at 70mph on a three-lane motorway. There is no traffic ahead. Which lane should you use?

Mark one answer

- A. Any lane
- B. Middle lane
- C. Right lane
- D. Left lane

568
Your vehicle has broken down on a motorway. You are not able to stop on the hard shoulder. What should you do?

Mark one answer

- A. Switch on your hazard warning lights
- B. Stop following traffic and ask for help
- C. Attempt to repair your vehicle quickly
- D. Stand behind your vehicle to warn others

569
Why is it particularly important to carry out a check on your vehicle before making a long motorway journey?

Mark one answer

- A. You will have to do more harsh braking on motorways
- B. Motorway service stations do not deal with breakdowns
- C. The road surface will wear down the tyres faster
- D. Continuous high speeds may increase the risk of your vehicle breaking down

570
For what reason may you use the right-hand lane of a motorway?

Mark one answer

- A. For keeping out of the way of lorries
- B. For travelling at more than 70mph
- C. For turning right
- D. For overtaking other vehicles

571
On a motorway you may ONLY stop on the hard shoulder

Mark one answer

- A. in an emergency
- B. if you feel tired and need to rest
- C. if you miss the exit that you wanted
- D. to pick up a hitchhiker

572
You are driving on a motorway. The car ahead shows its hazard lights for a short time. This tells you that

Mark one answer
- [ ] **A.** the driver wants you to overtake
- [ ] **B.** the other car is going to change lanes
- [ ] **C.** traffic ahead is slowing or stopping suddenly
- [ ] **D.** there is a police speed check ahead

573
Motorway emergency telephones are usually linked to the police. In some areas they are now linked to

Mark one answer
- [ ] **A.** the local ambulance service
- [ ] **B.** an Highways Agency control centre
- [ ] **C.** the local fire brigade
- [ ] **D.** a breakdown service control centre

574
You are intending to leave the motorway at the next exit. Before you reach the exit you should normally position your vehicle

Mark one answer
- [ ] **A.** in the middle lane
- [ ] **B.** in the left-hand lane
- [ ] **C.** on the hard shoulder
- [ ] **D.** in any lane

575
As a provisional licence holder you should not drive a car

Mark one answer
- [ ] **A.** over 30mph
- [ ] **B.** at night
- [ ] **C.** on the motorway
- [ ] **D.** with passengers in rear seats

576
Motorway emergency telephones are usually linked to the police. In some areas they are now linked to

NI

Mark one answer
- [ ] **A.** the Highways Agency Control Centre
- [ ] **B.** the Driver Vehicle Licensing Agency
- [ ] **C.** the Driving Standards Agency
- [ ] **D.** the local Vehicle Registration Office

577
An Emergency Refuge Area is an area

Mark one answer
- [ ] **A.** on a motorway for use in cases of emergency or breakdown
- [ ] **B.** for use if you think you will be involved in a road rage incident
- [ ] **C.** on a motorway for a police patrol to park and watch traffic
- [ ] **D.** for construction and road workers to store emergency equipment

578
What is an Emergency Refuge Area on a motorway for?

Mark one answer
- [ ] **A.** An area to park in when you want to use a mobile phone
- [ ] **B.** To use in cases of emergency or breakdown
- [ ] **C.** For an emergency recovery vehicle to park in a contraflow system
- [ ] **D.** To drive in when there is queuing traffic ahead

579
Highways Agency Traffic Officers

NI

Mark one answer
- [ ] **A.** will not be able to assist at a breakdown or emergency
- [ ] **B.** are not able to stop and direct anyone on a motorway
- [ ] **C.** will tow a broken down vehicle and its passengers home
- [ ] **D.** are able to stop and direct anyone on a motorway

580 You are on a motorway. A red cross is displayed above the hard shoulder. What does this mean?

Mark one answer **NI**

☐ **A.** Pull up in this lane to answer your mobile phone
☐ **B.** Use this lane as a running lane
☐ **C.** This lane can be used if you need a rest
☐ **D.** You should not travel in this lane

---

581 You are on a motorway in an Active Traffic Management (ATM) area. A mandatory speed limit is displayed above the hard shoulder. What does this mean?

Mark one answer **NI**

☐ **A.** You should not travel in this lane
☐ **B.** The hard shoulder can be used as a running lane
☐ **C.** You can park on the hard shoulder if you feel tired
☐ **D.** You can pull up in this lane to answer a mobile phone

---

582 The aim of an Active Traffic Management scheme on a motorway is to

Mark one answer **NI**

☐ **A.** prevent overtaking
☐ **B.** reduce rest stops
☐ **C.** prevent tailgating
☐ **D.** reduce congestion

---

583 You are in an Active Traffic Management area on a motorway. When the Actively Managed mode is operating

Mark one answer **NI**

☐ **A.** speed limits are only advisory
☐ **B.** the national speed limit will apply
☐ **C.** the speed limit is always 30mph
☐ **D.** all speed limit signals are set

---

584 You are on a three-lane motorway. A red cross is shown above the hard shoulder and mandatory speed limits above all other lanes. This means

Mark one answer **NI**

☐ **A.** the hard shoulder can be used as a rest area if you feel tired
☐ **B.** the hard shoulder is for emergency or breakdown use only
☐ **C.** the hard shoulder can be used as a normal running lane
☐ **D.** the hard shoulder has a speed limit of 50mph

585
You are travelling on a motorway. A red cross is shown above the hard shoulder. What does this mean?

Mark one answer **NI**
- [ ] A. Use this lane as a rest area
- [ ] B. Use this as a normal running lane
- [ ] C. Do not use this lane to travel in
- [ ] D. National speed limit applies in this lane

586
You are on a three-lane motorway and see this sign. It means you can use

Mark one answer **NI**
- [ ] A. any lane except the hard shoulder
- [ ] B. the hard shoulder only
- [ ] C. the three right hand lanes only
- [ ] D. all the lanes including the hard shoulder

587
Why can it be an advantage for traffic speed to stay constant over a longer distance?

Mark one answer
- [ ] A. You will do more stop-start driving
- [ ] B. You will use far more fuel
- [ ] C. You will be able to use more direct routes
- [ ] D. Your overall journey time will normally improve

588
You should not normally travel on the hard shoulder of a motorway. When can you use it?

Mark one answer **NI**
- [ ] A. When taking the next exit
- [ ] B. When traffic is stopped
- [ ] C. When signs direct you to
- [ ] D. When traffic is slow moving

589
On a motorway what is used to reduce traffic bunching?

Mark one answer
- [ ] A. Variable speed limits
- [ ] B. Contraflow systems
- [ ] C. National speed limits
- [ ] D. Lane closures

590
When may you stop on a motorway?

Mark one answer
- [ ] A. If you have to read a map
- [ ] B. When you are tired and need a rest
- [ ] C. If your mobile phone rings
- [ ] D. In an emergency or breakdown

591
You are travelling on a motorway. You decide you need a rest. You should

Mark one answer
- [ ] A. stop on the hard shoulder
- [ ] B. pull in at the nearest service area
- [ ] C. pull up on a slip road
- [ ] D. park on the central reservation

592 What is the meaning of this sign?

Mark one answer

- **A.** Local speed limit applies
- **B.** No waiting on the carriageway
- **C.** National speed limit applies
- **D.** No entry to vehicular traffic

593 What is the national speed limit on a single carriageway road for cars and motorcycles?

Mark one answer

- **A.** 30mph
- **B.** 50mph
- **C.** 60mph
- **D.** 70mph

594 What is the national speed limit for cars and motorcycles on a dual carriageway?

Mark one answer

- **A.** 30mph
- **B.** 50mph
- **C.** 60mph
- **D.** 70mph

595 There are no speed limit signs on the road. How is a 30mph limit indicated?

Mark one answer

- **A.** By hazard warning lines
- **B.** By street lighting
- **C.** By pedestrian islands
- **D.** By double or single yellow lines

596 Where you see street lights but no speed limit signs the limit is usually

Mark one answer

- **A.** 30mph
- **B.** 40mph
- **C.** 50mph
- **D.** 60mph

597 What does this sign mean?

Mark one answer

- **A.** Minimum speed 30mph
- **B.** End of maximum speed
- **C.** End of minimum speed
- **D.** Maximum speed 30mph

598 There is a tractor ahead of you. You wish to overtake but you are NOT sure if it is safe to do so. You should

Mark one answer

- **A.** follow another overtaking vehicle through
- **B.** sound your horn to the slow vehicle to pull over
- **C.** speed through but flash your lights to oncoming traffic
- **D.** not overtake if you are in doubt

599 Which three of the following are most likely to take an unusual course at roundabouts?

Mark three answers

- **A.** Horse riders
- **B.** Milk floats
- **C.** Delivery vans
- **D.** Long vehicles
- **E.** Estate cars
- **F.** Cyclists

600
In which TWO places should you NOT park?

Mark two answers
- [ ] **A.** Near a school entrance
- [ ] **B.** Near a police station
- [ ] **C.** In a side road
- [ ] **D.** At a bus stop
- [ ] **E.** In a one-way street

601
On a clearway you must not stop

Mark one answer
- [ ] **A.** at any time
- [ ] **B.** when it is busy
- [ ] **C.** in the rush hour
- [ ] **D.** during daylight hours

602
What is the meaning of this sign?

Mark one answer
- [ ] **A.** No entry
- [ ] **B.** Waiting restrictions
- [ ] **C.** National speed limit
- [ ] **D.** School crossing patrol

603
You can park on the right-hand side of a road at night

Mark one answer
- [ ] **A.** in a one-way street
- [ ] **B.** with your sidelights on
- [ ] **C.** more than 10 metres (32 feet) from a junction
- [ ] **D.** under a lamp-post

604
On a three-lane dual carriageway the right-hand lane can be used for

Mark one answer
- [ ] **A.** overtaking only, never turning right
- [ ] **B.** overtaking or turning right
- [ ] **C.** fast-moving traffic only
- [ ] **D.** turning right only, never overtaking

605
You are approaching a busy junction. There are several lanes with road markings. At the last moment you realise that you are in the wrong lane. You should

Mark one answer
- [ ] **A.** continue in that lane
- [ ] **B.** force your way across
- [ ] **C.** stop until the area has cleared
- [ ] **D.** use clear arm signals to cut across

606
Where may you overtake on a one-way street?

Mark one answer
- [ ] **A.** Only on the left-hand side
- [ ] **B.** Overtaking is not allowed
- [ ] **C.** Only on the right-hand side
- [ ] **D.** Either on the right or the left

607
When going straight ahead at a roundabout you should

Mark one answer
- [ ] **A.** indicate left before leaving the roundabout
- [ ] **B.** not indicate at any time
- [ ] **C.** indicate right when approaching the roundabout
- [ ] **D.** indicate left when approaching the roundabout

608 Which vehicle might have to use a different course to normal at roundabouts?

Mark one answer
- **A.** Sports car
- **B.** Van
- **C.** Estate car
- **D.** Long vehicle

609 You are going straight ahead at a roundabout. How should you signal?

Mark one answer
- **A.** Signal right on the approach and then left to leave the roundabout
- **B.** Signal left after you leave the roundabout and enter the new road
- **C.** Signal right on the approach to the roundabout and keep the signal on
- **D.** Signal left just after you pass the exit before the one you will take

610 You may only enter a box junction when

Mark one answer
- **A.** there are less than two vehicles in front of you
- **B.** the traffic lights show green
- **C.** your exit road is clear
- **D.** you need to turn left

611 You may wait in a yellow box junction when

Mark one answer
- **A.** oncoming traffic is preventing you from turning right
- **B.** you are in a queue of traffic turning left
- **C.** you are in a queue of traffic to go ahead
- **D.** you are on a roundabout

612 You MUST stop when signalled to do so by which THREE of these?

Mark three answers
- **A.** A police officer
- **B.** A pedestrian
- **C.** A school crossing patrol
- **D.** A bus driver
- **E.** A red traffic light

613 You will see these red and white markers when approaching

Mark one answer
- **A.** the end of a motorway
- **B.** a concealed level crossing
- **C.** a concealed speed limit sign
- **D.** the end of a dual carriageway

614 Someone is waiting to cross at a zebra crossing. They are standing on the pavement. You should normally

Mark one answer

- A. go on quickly before they step on to the crossing
- B. stop before you reach the zigzag lines and let them cross
- C. stop, let them cross, wait patiently
- D. ignore them as they are still on the pavement

615 At toucan crossings, apart from pedestrians you should be aware of

Mark one answer

- A. emergency vehicles emerging
- B. buses pulling out
- C. trams crossing in front
- D. cyclists riding across

616 Who can use a toucan crossing?

Mark two answers

- A. Trains
- B. Cyclists
- C. Buses
- D. Pedestrians
- E. Trams

617 At a pelican crossing, what does a flashing amber light mean?

Mark one answer

- A. You must not move off until the lights stop flashing
- B. You must give way to pedestrians still on the crossing
- C. You can move off, even if pedestrians are still on the crossing
- D. You must stop because the lights are about to change to red

618 You are waiting at a pelican crossing. The red light changes to flashing amber. This means you must

Mark one answer

- A. wait for pedestrians on the crossing to clear
- B. move off immediately without any hesitation
- C. wait for the green light before moving off
- D. get ready and go when the continuous amber light shows

619 You are travelling on a well-lit road at night in a built-up area. By using dipped headlights you will be able to

Mark one answer

- A. see further along the road
- B. go at a much faster speed
- C. switch to main beam quickly
- D. be easily seen by others

620 When can you park on the left opposite these road markings?

Mark one answer

- A. If the line nearest to you is broken
- B. When there are no yellow lines
- C. To pick up or set down passengers
- D. During daylight hours only

621
You are intending to turn right at a crossroads. An oncoming driver is also turning right. It will normally be safer to

Mark one answer

- **A.** keep the other vehicle to your RIGHT and turn behind it (offside to offside)
- **B.** keep the other vehicle to your LEFT and turn in front of it (nearside to nearside)
- **C.** carry on and turn at the next junction instead
- **D.** hold back and wait for the other driver to turn first

622
You are on a road that has no traffic signs. There are street lights. What is the speed limit?

Mark one answer

- **A.** 20mph
- **B.** 30mph
- **C.** 40mph
- **D.** 60mph

623
You are going along a street with parked vehicles on the left-hand side. For which THREE reasons should you keep your speed down?

Mark three answers

- **A.** So that oncoming traffic can see you more clearly
- **B.** You may set off car alarms
- **C.** Vehicles may be pulling out
- **D.** Drivers' doors may open
- **E.** Children may run out from between the vehicles

624
You meet an obstruction on your side of the road. You should

Mark one answer

- **A.** carry on, you have priority
- **B.** give way to oncoming traffic
- **C.** wave oncoming vehicles through
- **D.** accelerate to get past first

625
You are on a two-lane dual carriageway. For which TWO of the following would you use the right-hand lane?

Mark two answers

- **A.** Turning right
- **B.** Normal progress
- **C.** Staying at the minimum allowed speed
- **D.** Constant high speed
- **E.** Overtaking slower traffic
- **F.** Mending punctures

626
Who has priority at an unmarked crossroads?

Mark one answer

- **A.** The larger vehicle
- **B.** No one has priority
- **C.** The faster vehicle
- **D.** The smaller vehicle

627
What is the nearest you may park to a junction?

Mark one answer **NI**

- **A.** 10 metres (32 feet)
- **B.** 12 metres (39 feet)
- **C.** 15 metres (49 feet)
- **D.** 20 metres (66 feet)

628
In which THREE places must you NOT park?

Mark three answers **NI**

- **A.** Near the brow of a hill
- **B.** At or near a bus stop
- **C.** Where there is no pavement
- **D.** Within 10 metres (32 feet) of a junction
- **E.** On a 40mph road

629 You are waiting at a level crossing. A train has passed but the lights keep flashing. You must

Mark one answer
- A. carry on waiting
- B. phone the signal operator
- C. edge over the stop line and look for trains
- D. park and investigate

630 You park at night on a road with a 40mph speed limit. You should park

Mark one answer
- A. facing the traffic
- B. with parking lights on
- C. with dipped headlights on
- D. near a street light

631 The dual carriageway you are turning right on to has a very narrow central reservation. What should you do?

Mark one answer
- A. Proceed to the central reservation and wait
- B. Wait until the road is clear in both directions
- C. Stop in the first lane so that other vehicles give way
- D. Emerge slightly to show your intentions

632 At a crossroads there are no signs or road markings. Two vehicles approach. Which has priority?

Mark one answer
- A. Neither of the vehicles
- B. The vehicle travelling the fastest
- C. Oncoming vehicles turning right
- D. Vehicles approaching from the right

633 What does this sign tell you?

Mark one answer
- A. That it is a no-through road
- B. End of traffic calming zone
- C. Free parking zone ends
- D. No waiting zone ends

634 You are entering an area of road works. There is a temporary speed limit displayed. You should

Mark one answer
- A. not exceed the speed limit
- B. obey the limit only during rush hour
- C. ignore the displayed limit
- D. obey the limit except at night

635 You may drive over a footpath

Mark one answer
- A. to overtake slow-moving traffic
- B. when the pavement is very wide
- C. if no pedestrians are near
- D. to get into a property

636 A single-carriageway road has this sign. What is the maximum permitted speed for a car towing a trailer?

Mark one answer

- A. 30mph
- B. 40mph
- C. 50mph
- D. 60mph

637 You are towing a small caravan on a dual carriageway. You must not exceed

Mark one answer

- A. 50mph
- B. 40mph
- C. 70mph
- D. 60mph

638 You want to park and you see this sign. On the days and times shown you should

Mark one answer

- A. park in a bay and not pay
- B. park on yellow lines and pay
- C. park on yellow lines and not pay
- D. park in a bay and pay

Meter
ZONE

Mon - Fri
8.30 am - 6.30 pm
Saturday
8.30 am - 1.30 pm

639 You are driving along a road that has a cycle lane. The lane is marked by a solid white line. This means that during its period of operation

Mark one answer

- A. the lane may be used for parking your car
- B. you may drive in that lane at any time
- C. the lane may be used when necessary
- D. you must not drive in that lane

640 A cycle lane is marked by a solid white line. You must not drive or park in it

Mark one answer

- A. at any time
- B. during the rush hour
- C. if a cyclist is using it
- D. during its period of operation

641 While driving, you intend to turn left into a minor road. On the approach you should

Mark one answer

- A. keep just left of the middle of the road
- B. keep in the middle of the road
- C. swing out wide just before turning
- D. keep well to the left of the road

642 You are waiting at a level crossing. The red warning lights continue to flash after a train has passed by. What should you do?

Mark one answer

- A. Get out and investigate
- B. Telephone the signal operator
- C. Continue to wait
- D. Drive across carefully

643 You are driving over a level crossing. The warning lights come on and a bell rings. What should you do?

Mark one answer

- A. Get everyone out of the vehicle immediately
- B. Stop and reverse back to clear the crossing
- C. Keep going and clear the crossing
- D. Stop immediately and use your hazard warning lights

644 You are on a busy main road and find that you are travelling in the wrong direction. What should you do?

Mark one answer

- A. Turn into a side road on the right and reverse into the main road
- B. Make a U-turn in the main road
- C. Make a 'three-point' turn in the main road
- D. Turn round in a side road

645 You may remove your seat belt when carrying out a manoeuvre that involves

Mark one answer

- A. reversing
- B. a hill start
- C. an emergency stop
- D. driving slowly

646 You must not reverse

Mark one answer

- A. for longer than necessary
- B. for more than a car's length
- C. into a side road
- D. in a built-up area

647 You are parked in a busy high street. What is the safest way to turn your vehicle around so you can go the opposite way?

Mark one answer

- A. Find a quiet side road to turn round in
- B. Drive into a side road and reverse into the main road
- C. Get someone to stop the traffic
- D. Do a U-turn

648 When you are NOT sure that it is safe to reverse your vehicle you should

Mark one answer

- [ ] **A.** use your horn
- [ ] **B.** rev your engine
- [ ] **C.** get out and check
- [ ] **D.** reverse slowly

649 When may you reverse from a side road into a main road?

Mark one answer

- [ ] **A.** Only if both roads are clear of traffic
- [ ] **B.** Not at any time
- [ ] **C.** At any time
- [ ] **D.** Only if the main road is clear of traffic

650 You want to turn right at a box junction. There is oncoming traffic. You should

Mark one answer

- [ ] **A.** wait in the box junction if your exit is clear
- [ ] **B.** wait before the junction until it is clear of all traffic
- [ ] **C.** drive on, you cannot turn right at a box junction
- [ ] **D.** drive slowly into the box junction when signalled by oncoming traffic

651 You are reversing your vehicle into a side road. When would the greatest hazard to passing traffic occur?

Mark one answer

- [ ] **A.** After you've completed the manoeuvre
- [ ] **B.** Just before you actually begin to manoeuvre
- [ ] **C.** After you've entered the side road
- [ ] **D.** When the front of your vehicle swings out

652 You are driving on a road that has a cycle lane. The lane is marked by a broken white line. This means that

Mark two answers

- [ ] **A.** you should not drive in the lane unless it is unavoidable
- [ ] **B.** you should not park in the lane unless it is unavoidable
- [ ] **C.** cyclists can travel in both directions in that lane
- [ ] **D.** the lane must be used by motorcyclists in heavy traffic

653 Where is the safest place to park your vehicle at night?

Mark one answer

- [ ] **A.** In a garage
- [ ] **B.** On a busy road
- [ ] **C.** In a quiet car park
- [ ] **D.** Near a red route

654 To help keep your vehicle secure at night where should you park?

Mark one answer

- [ ] **A.** Near a police station
- [ ] **B.** In a quiet road
- [ ] **C.** On a red route
- [ ] **D.** In a well-lit area

655 You are in the right-hand lane of a dual carriageway. You see signs showing that the right-hand lane is closed 800 yards ahead. You should

GET IN LANE

↑ ↑ ⊤

800 yards

Mark one answer

- A. keep in that lane until you reach the queue
- B. move to the left immediately
- C. wait and see which lane is moving faster
- D. move to the left in good time

656 You are driving on an urban clearway. You may stop only to

Mark one answer

- A. set down and pick up passengers
- B. use a mobile telephone
- C. ask for directions
- D. load or unload goods

657 You are looking for somewhere to park your vehicle. The area is full EXCEPT for spaces marked 'disabled use'. You can

Mark one answer

- A. use these spaces when elsewhere is full
- B. park if you stay with your vehicle
- C. use these spaces, disabled or not
- D. not park there unless permitted

658 Your vehicle is parked on the road at night. When must you use sidelights?

Mark one answer

- A. Where there are continuous white lines in the middle of the road
- B. Where the speed limit exceeds 30mph
- C. Where you are facing oncoming traffic
- D. Where you are near a bus stop

659 On which THREE occasions MUST you stop your vehicle?

Mark three answers

- A. When in an accident where damage or injury is caused
- B. At a red traffic light
- C. When signalled to do so by a police or traffic officer
- D. At a junction with double broken white lines
- E. At a pelican crossing when the amber light is flashing and no pedestrians are crossing

660 You are on a road that is only wide enough for one vehicle. There is a car coming towards you. What should you do?

Mark one answer

- A. Pull into a passing place on your right
- B. Force the other driver to reverse
- C. Pull into a passing place if your vehicle is wider
- D. Pull into a passing place on your left

661 What MUST you have to park in a disabled space?

Mark one answer

- [ ] **A.** A Blue Badge
- [ ] **B.** A wheelchair
- [ ] **C.** An advanced driver certificate
- [ ] **D.** An adapted vehicle

662 You are driving at night with full beam headlights on. A vehicle is overtaking you. You should dip your lights

Mark one answer

- [ ] **A.** some time after the vehicle has passed you
- [ ] **B.** before the vehicle starts to pass you
- [ ] **C.** only if the other driver dips their headlights
- [ ] **D.** as soon as the vehicle passes you

663 When may you drive a motor car in this bus lane?

local | taxi

Mon - Fri
7 - 10 am
4.00 - 6.30 pm

Mark one answer

- [ ] **A.** Outside its hours of operation
- [ ] **B.** To get to the front of a traffic queue
- [ ] **C.** You may not use it at any time
- [ ] **D.** To overtake slow-moving traffic

664 Signals are normally given by direction indicators and

Mark one answer

- [ ] **A.** brake lights
- [ ] **B.** sidelights
- [ ] **C.** fog lights
- [ ] **D.** interior lights

665 You are travelling on a motorway. You MUST stop when signalled to do so by which of these?

Mark one answer   **NI**

- [ ] **A.** Flashing amber lights above your lane
- [ ] **B.** A Highways Agency Traffic Officer
- [ ] **C.** Pedestrians on the hard shoulder
- [ ] **D.** A driver who has broken down

666 At a busy unmarked crossroads, which of the following has priority?

Mark one answer

- [ ] **A.** Vehicles going straight ahead
- [ ] **B.** Vehicles turning right
- [ ] **C.** None of the vehicles
- [ ] **D.** The vehicles that arrived first

667 You MUST obey signs giving orders. These signs are mostly in

Mark one answer

- **A.** green rectangles
- **B.** red triangles
- **C.** blue rectangles
- **D.** red circles

668 Traffic signs giving orders are generally which shape?

Mark one answer

- **A.**
- **B.**
- **C.**
- **D.**

669 Which type of sign tells you NOT to do something?

Mark one answer

- **A.**
- **B.**
- **C.**
- **D.**

670 What does this sign mean?

Mark one answer

- **A.** Maximum speed limit with traffic calming
- **B.** Minimum speed limit with traffic calming
- **C.** '20 cars only' parking zone
- **D.** Only 20 cars allowed at any one time

671 Which sign means no motor vehicles are allowed?

Mark one answer

- **A.**
- **B.**
- **C.**
- **D.**

672 Which of these signs means no motor vehicles?

Mark one answer

- **A.**
- **B.**
- **C.**
- **D.**

673 What does this sign mean?

Mark one answer
- A. New speed limit 20mph
- B. No vehicles over 30 tonnes
- C. Minimum speed limit 30mph
- D. End of 20mph zone

674 What does this sign mean?

Mark one answer
- A. No overtaking
- B. No motor vehicles
- C. Clearway (no stopping)
- D. Cars and motorcycles only

675 What does this sign mean?

Mark one answer
- A. No parking
- B. No road markings
- C. No through road
- D. No entry

676 What does this sign mean?

Mark one answer
- A. Bend to the right
- B. Road on the right closed
- C. No traffic from the right
- D. No right turn

677 Which sign means 'no entry'?

Mark one answer
- A.
- B.
- C.
- D.

678 What does this sign mean?

Mark one answer
- A. Route for trams only
- B. Route for buses only
- C. Parking for buses only
- D. Parking for trams only

679 Which type of vehicle does this sign apply to?

Mark one answer

- A. Wide vehicles
- B. Long vehicles
- C. High vehicles
- D. Heavy vehicles

680 Which sign means NO motor vehicles allowed?

Mark one answer

A.

B.

C.

D.

681 What does this sign mean?

Mark one answer

- A. You have priority
- B. No motor vehicles
- C. Two-way traffic
- D. No overtaking

682 What does this sign mean?

Mark one answer

- A. Keep in one lane
- B. Give way to oncoming traffic
- C. Do not overtake
- D. Form two lanes

683 Which sign means no overtaking?

Mark one answer

A.

B.

C.

D.

684 What does this sign mean?

Mark one answer

- A. Waiting restrictions apply
- B. Waiting permitted
- C. National speed limit applies
- D. Clearway (no stopping)

685 What does this sign mean?

Mark one answer

- [ ] **A.** End of restricted speed area
- [ ] **B.** End of restricted parking area
- [ ] **C.** End of clearway
- [ ] **D.** End of cycle route

686 Which sign means 'no stopping'?

Mark one answer

- [ ] **A.**
- [ ] **B.**
- [ ] **C.**
- [ ] **D.**

687 What does this sign mean?

Mark one answer

- [ ] **A.** Roundabout
- [ ] **B.** Crossroads
- [ ] **C.** No stopping
- [ ] **D.** No entry

688 You see this sign ahead. It means

Mark one answer

- [ ] **A.** national speed limit applies
- [ ] **B.** waiting restrictions apply
- [ ] **C.** no stopping
- [ ] **D.** no entry

689 What does this sign mean?

Mark one answer

- [ ] **A.** Distance to parking place ahead
- [ ] **B.** Distance to public telephone ahead
- [ ] **C.** Distance to public house ahead
- [ ] **D.** Distance to passing place ahead

690 What does this sign mean?

Mark one answer

- [ ] **A.** Vehicles may not park on the verge or footway
- [ ] **B.** Vehicles may park on the left-hand side of the road only
- [ ] **C.** Vehicles may park fully on the verge or footway
- [ ] **D.** Vehicles may park on the right-hand side of the road only

691 What does this traffic sign mean?

Mark one answer
- [ ] **A.** No overtaking allowed
- [ ] **B.** Give priority to oncoming traffic
- [ ] **C.** Two-way traffic
- [ ] **D.** One-way traffic only

692 What is the meaning of this traffic sign?

Mark one answer
- [ ] **A.** End of two-way road
- [ ] **B.** Give priority to vehicles coming towards you
- [ ] **C.** You have priority over vehicles coming towards you
- [ ] **D.** Bus lane ahead

693 What MUST you do when you see this sign?

Mark one answer
- [ ] **A.** Stop, only if traffic is approaching
- [ ] **B.** Stop, even if the road is clear
- [ ] **C.** Stop, only if children are waiting to cross
- [ ] **D.** Stop, only if a red light is showing

694 What does this sign mean?

Mark one answer
- [ ] **A.** No overtaking
- [ ] **B.** You are entering a one-way street
- [ ] **C.** Two-way traffic ahead
- [ ] **D.** You have priority over vehicles from the opposite direction

695 What shape is a STOP sign at a junction?

Mark one answer
- [ ] **A.**
- [ ] **B.**
- [ ] **C.**
- [ ] **D.**

696 At a junction you see this sign partly covered by snow. What does it mean?

Mark one answer
- [ ] **A.** Crossroads
- [ ] **B.** Give way
- [ ] **C.** Stop
- [ ] **D.** Turn right

697 Which shape is used for a 'give way' sign?

Mark one answer

A.

B.

C.

D.

698 What does this sign mean?

Mark one answer

A. Service area 30 miles ahead

B. Maximum speed 30mph

C. Minimum speed 30mph

D. Lay-by 30 miles ahead

699 Which of these signs means turn left ahead?

Mark one answer

A.

B.

C.

D.

700 What does this sign mean?

Mark one answer

A. Buses turning

B. Ring road

C. Mini-roundabout

D. Keep right

701 What does this sign mean?

Mark one answer

A. Give way to oncoming vehicles

B. Approaching traffic passes you on both sides

C. Turn off at the next available junction

D. Pass either side to get to the same destination

702 What does this sign mean?

Mark one answer

A. Route for trams

B. Give way to trams

C. Route for buses

D. Give way to buses

703 What does a circular traffic sign with a blue background do?

Mark one answer

- A. Give warning of a motorway ahead
- B. Give directions to a car park
- C. Give motorway information
- D. Give an instruction

704 Which sign shows that traffic can only travel in one direction on the road you're on?

Mark one answer

- A.
- B.
- C.
- D.

705 Where would you see a contraflow bus and cycle lane?

Mark one answer

- A. On a dual carriageway
- B. On a roundabout
- C. On an urban motorway
- D. On a one-way street

706 What does this sign mean?

Mark one answer

- A. Bus station on the right
- B. Contraflow bus lane
- C. With-flow bus lane
- D. Give way to buses

707 What does this sign mean?

Mark one answer

- A. With-flow bus and cycle lane
- B. Contraflow bus and cycle lane
- C. No buses and cycles allowed
- D. No waiting for buses and cycles

708 What does a sign with a brown background show?

Mark one answer

- A. Tourist directions
- B. Primary roads
- C. Motorway routes
- D. Minor routes

709 This sign means

Mark one answer

- [ ] **A.** tourist attraction
- [ ] **B.** beware of trains
- [ ] **C.** level crossing
- [ ] **D.** beware of trams

710 What are triangular signs for?

Mark one answer

- [ ] **A.** To give warnings
- [ ] **B.** To give information
- [ ] **C.** To give orders
- [ ] **D.** To give directions

711 What does this sign mean?

Mark one answer

- [ ] **A.** Turn left ahead
- [ ] **B.** T-junction
- [ ] **C.** No through road
- [ ] **D.** Give way

712 What does this sign mean?

Mark one answer

- [ ] **A.** Multi-exit roundabout
- [ ] **B.** Risk of ice
- [ ] **C.** Six roads converge
- [ ] **D.** Place of historical interest

713 What does this sign mean?

Mark one answer

- [ ] **A.** Crossroads
- [ ] **B.** Level crossing with gate
- [ ] **C.** Level crossing without gate
- [ ] **D.** Ahead only

714 What does this sign mean?

Mark one answer

- [ ] **A.** Ring road
- [ ] **B.** Mini-roundabout
- [ ] **C.** No vehicles
- [ ] **D.** Roundabout

715 Which FOUR of these would be indicated by a triangular road sign?

Mark four answers

- [ ] **A.** Road narrows
- [ ] **B.** Ahead only
- [ ] **C.** Low bridge
- [ ] **D.** Minimum speed
- [ ] **E.** Children crossing
- [ ] **F.** T-junction

716 What does this sign mean?

Mark one answer

- [ ] **A.** Cyclists must dismount
- [ ] **B.** Cycles are not allowed
- [ ] **C.** Cycle route ahead
- [ ] **D.** Cycle in single file

717 Which sign means that pedestrians may be walking along the road?

Mark one answer

- [ ] **A.**
- [ ] **B.**
- [ ] **C.**
- [ ] **D.**

718 Which of these signs warn you of a zebra crossing?

Mark one answer

- [ ] **A.**
- [ ] **B.**
- [ ] **C.**
- [ ] **D.**

719 What does this sign mean?

Mark one answer

- [ ] **A.** No footpath ahead
- [ ] **B.** Pedestrians only ahead
- [ ] **C.** Pedestrian crossing ahead
- [ ] **D.** School crossing ahead

720 What does this sign mean?

Mark one answer

- [ ] **A.** School crossing patrol
- [ ] **B.** No pedestrians allowed
- [ ] **C.** Pedestrian zone – no vehicles
- [ ] **D.** Zebra crossing ahead

721 Which of these signs means there is a double bend ahead?

Mark one answer

- [ ] A.
- [ ] B.
- [ ] C.
- [ ] D.

722 What does this sign mean?

Mark one answer

- [ ] A. Wait at the barriers
- [ ] B. Wait at the crossroads
- [ ] C. Give way to trams
- [ ] D. Give way to farm vehicles

723 What does this sign mean?

Mark one answer

- [ ] A. Humpback bridge
- [ ] B. Humps in the road
- [ ] C. Entrance to tunnel
- [ ] D. Soft verges

724 What does this sign mean?

Mark one answer

- [ ] A. Low bridge ahead
- [ ] B. Tunnel ahead
- [ ] C. Ancient monument ahead
- [ ] D. Traffic danger spot ahead

725 What does this sign mean?

Mark one answer

- [ ] A. Two-way traffic straight ahead
- [ ] B. Two-way traffic crosses a one-way road
- [ ] C. Two-way traffic over a bridge
- [ ] D. Two-way traffic crosses a two-way road

726 Which sign means there will be two-way traffic crossing your route ahead?

Mark one answer

- [ ] A.
- [ ] B.
- [ ] C.
- [ ] D.

727 Which of these signs means the end of a dual carriageway?

Mark one answer

- [ ] A.
- [ ] B.
- [ ] C.
- [ ] D.

728 What does this sign mean?

Mark one answer

- [ ] A. End of dual carriageway
- [ ] B. Tall bridge
- [ ] C. Road narrows
- [ ] D. End of narrow bridge

729 What does this sign mean?

Mark one answer

- [ ] A. Two-way traffic ahead across a one-way road
- [ ] B. Traffic approaching you has priority
- [ ] C. Two-way traffic straight ahead
- [ ] D. Motorway contraflow system ahead

730 What does this sign mean?

Mark one answer

- [ ] A. Crosswinds
- [ ] B. Road noise
- [ ] C. Airport
- [ ] D. Adverse camber

731 What does this traffic sign mean?

Mark one answer

- [ ] A. Slippery road ahead
- [ ] B. Tyres liable to punctures ahead
- [ ] C. Danger ahead
- [ ] D. Service area ahead

732 You are about to overtake when you see this sign. You should

Mark one answer

- [ ] A. overtake the other driver as quickly as possible
- [ ] B. move to the right to get a better view
- [ ] C. switch your headlights on before overtaking
- [ ] D. hold back until you can see clearly ahead

Hidden dip

733 What does this sign mean?

Mark one answer

- **A.** Level crossing with gate or barrier
- **B.** Gated road ahead
- **C.** Level crossing without gate or barrier
- **D.** Cattle grid ahead

734 What does this sign mean?

Mark one answer

- **A.** No trams ahead
- **B.** Oncoming trams
- **C.** Trams crossing ahead
- **D.** Trams only

735 What does this sign mean?

Mark one answer

- **A.** Adverse camber
- **B.** Steep hill downwards
- **C.** Uneven road
- **D.** Steep hill upwards

736 What does this sign mean?

Mark one answer

- **A.** Uneven road surface
- **B.** Bridge over the road
- **C.** Road ahead ends
- **D.** Water across the road

737 What does this sign mean?

Mark one answer

- **A.** Humpback bridge
- **B.** Traffic calming hump
- **C.** Low bridge
- **D.** Uneven road

738 What does this sign mean?

Mark one answer

- **A.** Turn left for parking area
- **B.** No through road on the left
- **C.** No entry for traffic turning left
- **D.** Turn left for ferry terminal

739 What does this sign mean?

Mark one answer
- [ ] **A.** T-junction
- [ ] **B.** No through road
- [ ] **C.** Telephone box ahead
- [ ] **D.** Toilet ahead

740 Which sign means 'no through road'?

Mark one answer
- [ ] **A.**
- [ ] **B.**
- [ ] **C.**
- [ ] **D.**

741 Which of the following signs informs you that you are coming to a 'no through road'?

Mark one answer
- [ ] **A.**
- [ ] **B.**
- [ ] **C.**
- [ ] **D.**

742 What does this sign mean?

Mark one answer
- [ ] **A.** Direction to park-and-ride car park
- [ ] **B.** No parking for buses or coaches
- [ ] **C.** Directions to bus and coach park
- [ ] **D.** Parking area for cars and coaches

743 You are in a tunnel and you see this sign. What does it mean?

Mark one answer
- [ ] **A.** Direction to emergency pedestrian exit
- [ ] **B.** Beware of pedestrians, no footpath ahead
- [ ] **C.** No access for pedestrians
- [ ] **D.** Beware of pedestrians crossing ahead

744 Which is the sign for a ring road?

Mark one answer
- [ ] **A.**
- [ ] **B.**
- [ ] **C.**
- [ ] **D.**

745

At a railway level crossing the red light signal continues to flash after a train has gone by. What should you do?

Mark one answer

- A. Phone the signal operator
- B. Alert drivers behind you
- C. Wait
- D. Proceed with caution

746

At a junction you see this signal. It means

Mark one answer

- A. cars must stop
- B. trams must stop
- C. both trams and cars must stop
- D. both trams and cars can continue

747

What does this sign mean?

Mark one answer

- A. The right-hand lane ahead is narrow
- B. Right-hand lane for buses only
- C. Right-hand lane for turning right
- D. The right-hand lane is closed

748

What does this sign mean?

Mark one answer

- A. Change to the left lane
- B. Leave at the next exit
- C. Contraflow system
- D. One-way street

749

What does this sign mean?

Mark one answer

- A. Leave motorway at next exit
- B. Lane for heavy and slow vehicles
- C. All lorries use the hard shoulder
- D. Rest area for lorries

750

You are approaching a red traffic light. What will the signal show next?

Mark one answer

- A. Red and amber
- B. Green alone
- C. Amber alone
- D. Green and amber

751 A red traffic light means

Mark one answer

- [ ] **A.** you should stop unless turning left
- [ ] **B.** stop, if you are able to brake safely
- [ ] **C.** you must stop and wait behind the stop line
- [ ] **D.** proceed with caution

752 At traffic lights, amber on its own means

Mark one answer

- [ ] **A.** prepare to go
- [ ] **B.** go if the way is clear
- [ ] **C.** go if no pedestrians are crossing
- [ ] **D.** stop at the stop line

753 You are approaching traffic lights. Red and amber are showing. This means

Mark one answer

- [ ] **A.** pass the lights if the road is clear
- [ ] **B.** there is a fault with the lights – take care
- [ ] **C.** wait for the green light before you cross the stop line
- [ ] **D.** the lights are about to change to red

754 You are at a junction controlled by traffic lights. When should you NOT proceed at green?

Mark one answer

- [ ] **A.** When pedestrians are waiting to cross
- [ ] **B.** When your exit from the junction is blocked
- [ ] **C.** When you think the lights may be about to change
- [ ] **D.** When you intend to turn right

755 You are in the left-hand lane at traffic lights. You are waiting to turn left. At which of these traffic lights must you NOT move on?

Mark one answer

- [ ] **A.**
- [ ] **B.**
- [ ] **C.**
- [ ] **D.**

756 What does this sign mean?

Mark one answer

- [ ] **A.** Traffic lights out of order
- [ ] **B.** Amber signal out of order
- [ ] **C.** Temporary traffic lights ahead
- [ ] **D.** New traffic lights ahead

757 When traffic lights are out of order, who has priority?

Mark one answer
- A. Traffic going straight on
- B. Traffic turning right
- C. Nobody
- D. Traffic turning left

758 These flashing red lights mean STOP. In which THREE of the following places could you find them?

Mark three answers
- A. Pelican crossings
- B. Lifting bridges
- C. Zebra crossings
- D. Level crossings
- E. Motorway exits
- F. Fire stations

759 What do these zigzag lines at pedestrian crossings mean?

Mark one answer
- A. No parking at any time
- B. Parking allowed only for a short time
- C. Slow down to 20mph
- D. Sounding horns is not allowed

760 When may you cross a double solid white line in the middle of the road?

Mark one answer
- A. To pass traffic that is queuing back at a junction
- B. To pass a car signalling to turn left ahead
- C. To pass a road maintenance vehicle travelling at 10mph or less
- D. To pass a vehicle that is towing a trailer

761 What does this road marking mean?

Mark one answer
- A. Do not cross the line
- B. No stopping allowed
- C. You are approaching a hazard
- D. No overtaking allowed

762 This marking appears on the road just before a

Mark one answer
- A. 'no entry' sign
- B. 'give way' sign
- C. 'stop' sign
- D. 'no through road' sign

763 Where would you see this road marking?

Mark one answer
- A. At traffic lights
- B. On road humps
- C. Near a level crossing
- D. At a box junction

764 Which is a hazard warning line?

Mark one answer
- A.

- B.

- C.

- D.

765 At this junction there is a stop sign with a solid white line on the road surface. Why is there a stop sign here?

Mark one answer
- A. Speed on the major road is de-restricted
- B. It is a busy junction
- C. Visibility along the major road is restricted
- D. There are hazard warning lines in the centre of the road

766 You see this line across the road at the entrance to a roundabout. What does it mean?

Mark one answer
- A. Give way to traffic from the right
- B. Traffic from the left has right of way
- C. You have right of way
- D. Stop at the line

767 Where would you find these road markings?

Mark one answer

- [ ] A. At a railway crossing
- [ ] B. At a junction
- [ ] C. On a motorway
- [ ] D. On a pedestrian crossing

768 How will a police officer in a patrol vehicle normally get you to stop?

Mark one answer

- [ ] A. Flash the headlights, indicate left and point to the left
- [ ] B. Wait until you stop, then approach you
- [ ] C. Use the siren, overtake, cut in front and stop
- [ ] D. Pull alongside you, use the siren and wave you to stop

769 There is a police car following you. The police officer flashes the headlights and points to the left. What should you do?

Mark one answer

- [ ] A. Turn left at the next junction
- [ ] B. Pull up on the left
- [ ] C. Stop immediately
- [ ] D. Move over to the left

770 The driver of the car in front is giving this arm signal. What does it mean?

Mark one answer

- [ ] A. The driver is slowing down
- [ ] B. The driver intends to turn right
- [ ] C. The driver wishes to overtake
- [ ] D. The driver intends to turn left

771 Where would you see these road markings?

Mark one answer

- [ ] A. At a level crossing
- [ ] B. On a motorway slip road
- [ ] C. At a pedestrian crossing
- [ ] D. On a single-track road

772 What does this motorway sign mean?

Mark one answer

- [ ] A. Change to the lane on your left
- [ ] B. Leave the motorway at the next exit
- [ ] C. Change to the opposite carriageway
- [ ] D. Pull up on the hard shoulder

773 What does this motorway sign mean?

Mark one answer

- [ ] **A.** Temporary minimum speed 50mph
- [ ] **B.** No services for 50 miles
- [ ] **C.** Obstruction 50 metres (164 feet) ahead
- [ ] **D.** Temporary maximum speed 50mph

774 What does this sign mean?

Mark one answer

- [ ] **A.** Through traffic to use left lane
- [ ] **B.** Right-hand lane T-junction only
- [ ] **C.** Right-hand lane closed ahead
- [ ] **D.** 11 tonne weight limit

775 On a motorway this sign means

Mark one answer

- [ ] **A.** move over on to the hard shoulder
- [ ] **B.** overtaking on the left only
- [ ] **C.** leave the motorway at the next exit
- [ ] **D.** move to the lane on your left

776 What does '25' mean on this motorway sign?

Mark one answer

- [ ] **A.** The distance to the nearest town
- [ ] **B.** The route number of the road
- [ ] **C.** The number of the next junction
- [ ] **D.** The speed limit on the slip road

777 The right-hand lane of a three-lane motorway is

Mark one answer

- [ ] **A.** for lorries only
- [ ] **B.** an overtaking lane
- [ ] **C.** the right-turn lane
- [ ] **D.** an acceleration lane

778 Where can you find reflective amber studs on a motorway?

Mark one answer

- [ ] **A.** Separating the slip road from the motorway
- [ ] **B.** On the left-hand edge of the road
- [ ] **C.** On the right-hand edge of the road
- [ ] **D.** Separating the lanes

779 Where on a motorway would you find green reflective studs?

Mark one answer
- A. Separating driving lanes
- B. Between the hard shoulder and the carriageway
- C. At slip road entrances and exits
- D. Between the carriageway and the central reservation

780 You are travelling along a motorway. You see this sign. You should

Mark one answer
- A. leave the motorway at the next exit
- B. turn left immediately
- C. change lane
- D. move on to the hard shoulder

781 What does this sign mean?

Mark one answer
- A. No motor vehicles
- B. End of motorway
- C. No through road
- D. End of bus lane

782 Which of these signs means that the national speed limit applies?

Mark one answer
- A.
- B.
- C.
- D.

783 What is the maximum speed on a single carriageway road?

Mark one answer
- A. 50mph
- B. 60mph
- C. 40mph
- D. 70mph

784 What does this sign mean?

End

Mark one answer
- A. End of motorway
- B. End of restriction
- C. Lane ends ahead
- D. Free recovery ends

785 This sign is advising you to

Mark one answer

- A. follow the route diversion
- B. follow the signs to the picnic area
- C. give way to pedestrians
- D. give way to cyclists

786 Why would this temporary speed limit sign be shown?

Mark one answer

- A. To warn of the end of the motorway
- B. To warn you of a low bridge
- C. To warn you of a junction ahead
- D. To warn of road works ahead

787 This traffic sign means there is

Mark one answer

- A. a compulsory maximum speed limit
- B. an advisory maximum speed limit
- C. a compulsory minimum speed limit
- D. an advised separation distance

788 You see this sign at a crossroads. You should

Mark one answer

- A. maintain the same speed
- B. carry on with great care
- C. find another route
- D. telephone the police

789 You are signalling to turn right in busy traffic. How would you confirm your intention safely?

Mark one answer

- A. Sound the horn
- B. Give an arm signal
- C. Flash your headlights
- D. Position over the centre line

790 What does this sign mean?

Mark one answer

- A. Motorcycles only
- B. No cars
- C. Cars only
- D. No motorcycles

791 You are on a motorway. You see this sign on a lorry that has stopped in the right-hand lane. You should

Mark one answer
- [ ] **A.** move into the right-hand lane
- [ ] **B.** stop behind the flashing lights
- [ ] **C.** pass the lorry on the left
- [ ] **D.** leave the motorway at the next exit

792 You are on a motorway. Red flashing lights appear above your lane only. What should you do?

Mark one answer
- [ ] **A.** Continue in that lane and look for further information
- [ ] **B.** Move into another lane in good time
- [ ] **C.** Pull on to the hard shoulder
- [ ] **D.** Stop and wait for an instruction to proceed

793 A red traffic light means

Mark one answer
- [ ] **A.** you must stop behind the white stop line
- [ ] **B.** you may go straight on if there is no other traffic
- [ ] **C.** you may turn left if it is safe to do so
- [ ] **D.** you must slow down and prepare to stop if traffic has started to cross

794 The driver of this car is giving an arm signal. What are they about to do?

Mark one answer
- [ ] **A.** Turn to the right
- [ ] **B.** Turn to the left
- [ ] **C.** Go straight ahead
- [ ] **D.** Let pedestrians cross

795 Which arm signal tells you that the car you are following is going to pull up?

Mark one answer
- [ ] **A.**
- [ ] **B.**
- [ ] **C.**
- [ ] **D.**

796 When may you sound the horn?

Mark one answer
- [ ] **A.** To give you right of way
- [ ] **B.** To attract a friend's attention
- [ ] **C.** To warn others of your presence
- [ ] **D.** To make slower drivers move over

797 You must not use your horn when you are stationary

Mark one answer

- [ ] **A.** unless a moving vehicle may cause you danger
- [ ] **B.** at any time whatsoever
- [ ] **C.** unless it is used only briefly
- [ ] **D.** except for signalling that you have just arrived

798 What does this sign mean?

URBAN CLEARWAY
Monday to Friday

am	pm
8.00 - 9.30	4.30 - 6.30

Mark one answer

- [ ] **A.** You can park on the days and times shown
- [ ] **B.** No parking on the days and times shown
- [ ] **C.** No parking at all from Monday to Friday
- [ ] **D.** End of the urban clearway restrictions

799 What does this sign mean?

Mark one answer

- [ ] **A.** Quayside or river bank
- [ ] **B.** Steep hill downwards
- [ ] **C.** Uneven road surface
- [ ] **D.** Road liable to flooding

800 You see this amber traffic light ahead. Which light or lights will come on next?

Mark one answer

- [ ] **A.** Red alone
- [ ] **B.** Red and amber together
- [ ] **C.** Green and amber together
- [ ] **D.** Green alone

801 This broken white line painted in the centre of the road means

Mark one answer

- [ ] **A.** oncoming vehicles have priority over you
- [ ] **B.** you should give priority to oncoming vehicles
- [ ] **C.** there is a hazard ahead of you
- [ ] **D.** the area is a national speed limit zone

802 Which sign means you have priority over oncoming vehicles?

Mark one answer

- [ ] **A.**
- [ ] **B.**
- [ ] **C.**
- [ ] **D.**

803 You see this signal overhead on the motorway. What does it mean?

Mark one answer

- [ ] **A.** Leave the motorway at the next exit
- [ ] **B.** All vehicles use the hard shoulder
- [ ] **C.** Sharp bend to the left ahead
- [ ] **D.** Stop, all lanes ahead closed

804 A white line like this along the centre of the road is a

Mark one answer

- [ ] **A.** bus lane marking
- [ ] **B.** hazard warning
- [ ] **C.** give way marking
- [ ] **D.** lane marking

805 What is the purpose of these yellow criss-cross lines on the road?

Mark one answer

- [ ] **A.** To make you more aware of the traffic lights
- [ ] **B.** To guide you into position as you turn
- [ ] **C.** To prevent the junction becoming blocked
- [ ] **D.** To show you where to stop when the lights change

806 What is the reason for the yellow criss-cross lines painted on the road here?

Mark one answer

- [ ] **A.** To mark out an area for trams only
- [ ] **B.** To prevent queuing traffic from blocking the junction on the left
- [ ] **C.** To mark the entrance lane to a car park
- [ ] **D.** To warn you of the tram lines crossing the road

807 What is the reason for the area marked in red and white along the centre of this road?

Mark one answer

- A. It is to separate traffic flowing in opposite directions
- B. It marks an area to be used by overtaking motorcyclists
- C. It is a temporary marking to warn of the roadworks
- D. It is separating the two sides of the dual carriageway

808 Other drivers may sometimes flash their headlights at you. In which situation are they allowed to do this?

Mark one answer

- A. To warn of a radar speed trap ahead
- B. To show that they are giving way to you
- C. To warn you of their presence
- D. To let you know there is a fault with your vehicle

809 You are approaching a zebra crossing where pedestrians are waiting. Which arm signal might you give?

Mark one answer

- A.
- B.
- C.
- D.

810 The white line along the side of the road

Mark one answer

- A. shows the edge of the carriageway
- B. shows the approach to a hazard
- C. means no parking
- D. means no overtaking

811 You see this white arrow on the road ahead. It means

Mark one answer

- A. entrance on the left
- B. all vehicles turn left
- C. keep left of the hatched markings
- D. road bending to the left

812 How should you give an arm signal to turn left?

Mark one answer

- A.
- B.
- C.
- D.

813
You are waiting at a T-junction. A vehicle is coming from the right with the left signal flashing. What should you do?

Mark one answer
- A. Move out and accelerate hard
- B. Wait until the vehicle starts to turn in
- C. Pull out before the vehicle reaches the junction
- D. Move out slowly

814
When may you use hazard warning lights when driving?

Mark one answer
- A. Instead of sounding the horn in a built-up area between 11.30pm and 7am
- B. On a motorway or unrestricted dual carriageway, to warn of a hazard ahead
- C. On rural routes, after a warning sign of animals
- D. On the approach to toucan crossings where cyclists are waiting to cross

815
You are driving on a motorway. There is a slow-moving vehicle ahead. On the back you see this sign. You should

Mark one answer
- A. pass on the right
- B. pass on the left
- C. leave at the next exit
- D. drive no further

816
In some narrow residential streets you may find a speed limit of

Mark one answer
- A. 20mph
- B. 25mph
- C. 35mph
- D. 40mph

817
You should NOT normally stop on these markings near schools

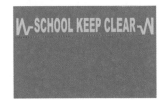

Mark one answer
- A. except when picking up children
- B. under any circumstances
- C. unless there is nowhere else available
- D. except to set down children

818 Why should you make sure that your indicators are cancelled after turning?

Mark one answer

- **A.** To avoid flattening the battery
- **B.** To avoid misleading other road users
- **C.** To avoid dazzling other road users
- **D.** To avoid damage to the indicator relay

819 You are driving in busy traffic. You want to pull up on the left just after a junction on the left. When should you signal?

Mark one answer

- **A.** As you are passing or just after the junction
- **B.** Just before you reach the junction
- **C.** Well before you reach the junction
- **D.** It would be better not to signal at all

820 You have just driven past this sign. You should be aware that

Mark one answer

- **A.** it is a single track road
- **B.** you cannot stop on this road
- **C.** there is only one lane in use
- **D.** all traffic is going one way

821 Which of these signs shows that you are entering a one-way system?

Mark one answer

- **A.**
- **B.**
- **C.**
- **D.**

822 You approach a junction. The traffic lights are not working. A police officer gives this signal. You should

Mark one answer

- **A.** turn left only
- **B.** turn right only
- **C.** stop level with the officer's arm
- **D.** stop at the stop line

823 An MOT certificate is normally valid for

Mark one answer

- A. three years after the date it was issued
- B. 10,000 miles
- C. one year after the date it was issued
- D. 30,000 miles

824 A cover note is a document issued before you receive your

Mark one answer

- A. driving licence
- B. insurance certificate
- C. registration document
- D. MOT certificate

825 A police officer asks to see your documents. You do not have them with you. You may be asked to take them to a police station within

Mark one answer

- A. 5 days
- B. 7 days
- C. 14 days
- D. 21 days

826 You have just passed your practical test. You do not hold a full licence in another category. Within two years you get six penalty points on your licence. What will you have to do?

Mark two answers

- A. Retake only your theory test
- B. Retake your theory and practical tests
- C. Retake only your practical test
- D. Reapply for your full licence immediately
- E. Reapply for your provisional licence

827 To drive on the road learners MUST

Mark one answer

- A. have NO penalty points on their licence
- B. have taken professional instruction
- C. have a signed, valid provisional licence
- D. apply for a driving test within 12 months

828 Before driving anyone else's motor vehicle you should make sure that

Mark one answer

- A. the vehicle owner has third party insurance cover
- B. your own vehicle has insurance cover
- C. the vehicle is insured for your use
- D. the owner has left the insurance documents in the vehicle

829 Your car needs an MOT certificate. If you drive without one this could invalidate your

Mark one answer

- A. vehicle service record
- B. insurance
- C. road tax disc
- D. vehicle registration document

830 When is it legal to drive a car over three years old without an MOT certificate?

Mark one answer **NI**

- A. Up to seven days after the old certificate has run out
- B. When driving to an MOT centre to arrange an appointment
- C. Just after buying a second-hand car with no MOT
- D. When driving to an appointment at an MOT centre

831 To supervise a learner driver you must

Mark two answers
- [ ] A. have held a full licence for at least 3 years
- [ ] B. be at least 21 years old
- [ ] C. be an approved driving instructor
- [ ] D. hold an advanced driving certificate

832 How old must you be to supervise a learner driver?

Mark one answer
- [ ] A. 18 years old
- [ ] B. 19 years old
- [ ] C. 20 years old
- [ ] D. 21 years old

833 A newly qualified driver must

Mark one answer
- [ ] A. display green 'L' plates
- [ ] B. not exceed 40mph for 12 months
- [ ] C. be accompanied on a motorway
- [ ] D. have valid motor insurance

834 You have third party insurance. What does this cover?

Mark three answers
- [ ] A. Damage to your own vehicle
- [ ] B. Damage to your vehicle by fire
- [ ] C. Injury to another person
- [ ] D. Damage to someone's property
- [ ] E. Damage to other vehicles
- [ ] F. Injury to yourself

835 For which of these MUST you show your insurance certificate?

Mark one answer
- [ ] A. When making a SORN declaration
- [ ] B. When buying or selling a vehicle
- [ ] C. When a police officer asks you for it
- [ ] D. When having an MOT inspection

836 Vehicle excise duty is often called 'Road Tax' or 'The Tax Disc'. You must

Mark one answer
- [ ] A. keep it with your registration document
- [ ] B. display it clearly on your vehicle
- [ ] C. keep it concealed safely in your vehicle
- [ ] D. carry it on you at all times

837 Motor cars must first have an MOT test certificate when they are

NI

Mark one answer
- [ ] A. one year old
- [ ] B. three years old
- [ ] C. five years old
- [ ] D. seven years old

838 Your vehicle needs a current MOT certificate. Until you have one you will NOT be able to

Mark one answer
- [ ] A. renew your driving licence
- [ ] B. change your insurance company
- [ ] C. renew your road tax disc
- [ ] D. notify a change of address

839 Which THREE pieces of information are found on a vehicle registration document?

Mark three answers
- [ ] A. Registered keeper
- [ ] B. Make of the vehicle
- [ ] C. Service history details
- [ ] D. Date of the MOT
- [ ] E. Type of insurance cover
- [ ] F. Engine size

840 You have a duty to contact the licensing authority when

Mark three answers

- A. you go abroad on holiday
- B. you change your vehicle
- C. you change your name
- D. your job status is changed
- E. your permanent address changes
- F. your job involves travelling abroad

841 You must notify the licensing authority when

Mark three answers

- A. your health affects your driving
- B. your eyesight does not meet a set standard
- C. you intend lending your vehicle
- D. your vehicle requires an MOT certificate
- E. you change your vehicle

842 Your vehicle is insured third party only. This covers

Mark two answers

- A. damage to your vehicle
- B. damage to other vehicles
- C. injury to yourself
- D. injury to others
- E. all damage and injury

843 Your motor insurance policy has an excess of £100. What does this mean?

Mark one answer

- A. The insurance company will pay the first £100 of any claim
- B. You will be paid £100 if you do not have a crash
- C. Your vehicle is insured for a value of £100 if it is stolen
- D. You will have to pay the first £100 of any claim

844 When you apply to renew your vehicle excise licence (tax disc) what must you have?

Mark one answer

- A. Valid insurance
- B. The old tax disc
- C. The vehicle handbook
- D. A valid driving licence

845 What is the legal minimum insurance cover you must have to drive on public roads?

Mark one answer

- A. Third party, fire and theft
- B. Comprehensive
- C. Third party only
- D. Personal injury cover

846 Which THREE of these do you need before you can drive legally?

Mark three answers

- A. A valid driving licence
- B. A valid tax disc displayed on your vehicle
- C. A vehicle service record
- D. Proper insurance cover
- E. Breakdown cover
- F. A vehicle handbook

847 The cost of your insurance may reduce if you

NI

Mark one answer

- A. are under 25 years old
- B. do not wear glasses
- C. pass the driving test first time
- D. take the Pass Plus scheme

848 Which of the following may reduce the cost of your insurance?

NI

Mark one answer

- A. Having a valid MOT certificate
- B. Taking a Pass Plus course
- C. Driving a powerful car
- D. Having penalty points on your licence

849 The Pass Plus scheme has been created for new drivers. What is its main purpose?

Mark one answer   **NI**

- [ ] A. To allow you to drive faster
- [ ] B. To allow you to carry passengers
- [ ] C. To improve your basic skills
- [ ] D. To let you drive on motorways

850 How long will a Statutory Off Road Notification (SORN) last for?

Mark one answer

- [ ] A. 12 months
- [ ] B. 24 months
- [ ] C. 3 years
- [ ] D. 10 years

851 What is a Statutory Off Road Notification (SORN) declaration?

Mark one answer   **NI**

- [ ] A. A notification to tell VOSA that a vehicle does not have a current MOT
- [ ] B. Information kept by the police about the owner of the vehicle
- [ ] C. A notification to tell DVLA that a vehicle is not being used on the road
- [ ] D. Information held by insurance companies to check the vehicle is insured

852 A Statutory Off Road Notification (SORN) declaration is

Mark one answer   **NI**

- [ ] A. to tell DVLA that your vehicle is being used on the road but the MOT has expired
- [ ] B. to tell DVLA that you no longer own the vehicle
- [ ] C. to tell DVLA that your vehicle is not being used on the road
- [ ] D. to tell DVLA that you are buying a personal number plate

853 You claim on your insurance to have your car repaired. Your policy has an excess of £100. What does this mean?

Mark one answer

- [ ] A. The insurance company will pay the first £100 of any claim
- [ ] B. You will be paid £100 if you do not claim within one year
- [ ] C. Your vehicle is insured for a value of £100 if it is stolen
- [ ] D. You will have to pay the first £100 of the cost of repair to your car

854 A Statutory Off Road Notification (SORN) is valid

Mark one answer

- [ ] A. for as long as the vehicle has an MOT
- [ ] B. for 12 months only
- [ ] C. only if the vehicle is more than 3 years old
- [ ] D. provided the vehicle is insured

855 A Statutory Off Road Notification (SORN) will last

Mark one answer

- [ ] A. for the life of the vehicle
- [ ] B. for as long as you own the vehicle
- [ ] C. for 12 months only
- [ ] D. until the vehicle warranty expires

856 What is the maximum specified fine for driving without insurance?

Mark one answer   **NI**

- [ ] A. £50
- [ ] B. £500
- [ ] C. £1,000
- [ ] D. £5,000

857 When should you update your Vehicle Registration Certificate?

Mark one answer
- A. When you pass your driving test
- B. When you move house
- C. When your vehicle needs an MOT
- D. When you have a collision

858 Who is legally responsible for ensuring that a Vehicle Registration Certificate (V5C) is updated?

Mark one answer
- A. The registered vehicle keeper
- B. The vehicle manufacturer
- C. Your insurance company
- D. The licensing authority

859 The Pass Plus scheme is designed to

Mark one answer NI
- A. give you a discount on your MOT
- B. improve your basic driving skills
- C. increase your mechanical knowledge
- D. allow you to drive anyone else's vehicle

860 By taking part in the Pass Plus scheme you will

Mark one answer NI
- A. never get any points on your licence
- B. be able to service your own car
- C. allow you to drive anyone else's vehicle
- D. improve your basic driving skills

861 The Pass Plus scheme is aimed at all newly qualified drivers. It enables them to

Mark one answer NI
- A. widen their driving experience
- B. supervise a learner driver
- C. increase their insurance premiums
- D. avoid mechanical breakdowns

862 New drivers can take further training after passing the practical test. A Pass Plus course will help to

Mark two answers NI
- A. improve your basic skills
- B. widen your experience
- C. increase your insurance premiums
- D. get cheaper road tax

863 The Pass Plus scheme is operated by DSA for newly qualified drivers. It is intended to

Mark one answer NI
- A. improve your basic skills
- B. reduce the cost of your driving licence
- C. prevent you from paying congestion charges
- D. allow you to supervise a learner driver

864 You must have valid insurance before you can

Mark one answer NI
- A. make a SORN declaration
- B. buy or sell a vehicle
- C. apply for a driving licence
- D. obtain a tax disc

865 A friend wants to help you learn to drive. They must be

Mark one answer NI
- A. at least 21 and have held a full licence for at least one year
- B. over 18 and hold an advanced driver's certificate
- C. over 18 and have fully comprehensive insurance
- D. at least 21 and have held a full licence for at least three years

866 Which THREE of these do you need before you can use a vehicle on the road legally?

Mark three answers

- [ ] **A.** A valid driving licence
- [ ] **B.** A valid tax disc clearly displayed
- [ ] **C.** Proof of your identity
- [ ] **D.** Proper insurance cover
- [ ] **E.** Breakdown cover
- [ ] **F.** A vehicle handbook

867 When you apply to renew your Vehicle Excise Duty (tax disc) you must have

Mark one answer

- [ ] **A.** valid insurance
- [ ] **B.** the old tax disc
- [ ] **C.** the handbook
- [ ] **D.** a valid driving licence

868 Your vehicle needs a current MOT certificate. You do not have one. Until you do have one you will not be able to renew your

Mark one answer

- [ ] **A.** driving licence
- [ ] **B.** vehicle insurance
- [ ] **C.** road tax disc
- [ ] **D.** vehicle registration document

869 For which of these must you show your motor insurance certificate?

Mark one answer

- [ ] **A.** When you are taking your driving test
- [ ] **B.** When buying or selling a vehicle
- [ ] **C.** When a police officer asks you for it
- [ ] **D.** When having an MOT inspection

870 At the scene of a traffic accident you should

Mark one answer

- [ ] **A.** not put yourself at risk
- [ ] **B.** go to those casualties who are screaming
- [ ] **C.** pull everybody out of their vehicles
- [ ] **D.** leave vehicle engines switched on

871 You are the first to arrive at the scene of a crash. Which TWO of these should you do?

Mark two answers

- [ ] **A.** Leave as soon as another motorist arrives
- [ ] **B.** Make sure engines are switched off
- [ ] **C.** Drag all casualties away from the vehicle
- [ ] **D.** Call the emergency services promptly

872 A collision has just happened. An injured person is lying in a busy road. What is the FIRST thing you should do to help?

Mark one answer

- [ ] **A.** Treat the person for shock
- [ ] **B.** Warn other traffic
- [ ] **C.** Place them in the recovery position
- [ ] **D.** Make sure the injured person is kept warm

873 You are the first person to arrive at an incident where people are badly injured. Which THREE should you do?

Mark three answers

- [ ] **A.** Switch on your own hazard warning lights
- [ ] **B.** Make sure that someone telephones for an ambulance
- [ ] **C.** Try and get people who are injured to drink something
- [ ] **D.** Move the people who are injured clear of their vehicles
- [ ] **E.** Get people who are not injured clear of the scene

874 You arrive at the scene of a motorcycle crash. The rider is injured. When should the helmet be removed?

Mark one answer

- [ ] **A.** Only when it is essential
- [ ] **B.** Always straight away
- [ ] **C.** Only when the motorcyclist asks
- [ ] **D.** Always, unless they are in shock

875 You arrive at a serious motorcycle crash. The motorcyclist is unconscious and bleeding. Your THREE main priorities should be to

Mark three answers

- [ ] **A.** try to stop the bleeding
- [ ] **B.** make a list of witnesses
- [ ] **C.** check their breathing
- [ ] **D.** take the numbers of other vehicles
- [ ] **E.** sweep up any loose debris
- [ ] **F.** check their airways

876 You arrive at an incident. A motorcyclist is unconscious. Your FIRST priority is the casualty's

Mark one answer

- [ ] **A.** breathing
- [ ] **B.** bleeding
- [ ] **C.** broken bones
- [ ] **D.** bruising

877 At an incident a casualty is unconscious. Which THREE of these should you check urgently?

Mark three answers

- [ ] **A.** Circulation
- [ ] **B.** Airway
- [ ] **C.** Shock
- [ ] **D.** Breathing
- [ ] **E.** Broken bones

878 You arrive at the scene of an incident. It has just happened and someone is unconscious. Which THREE of these should be given urgent priority to help them?

Mark three answers
- [ ] A. Clear the airway and keep it open
- [ ] B. Try to get them to drink water
- [ ] C. Check that they are breathing
- [ ] D. Look for any witnesses
- [ ] E. Stop any heavy bleeding
- [ ] F. Take the numbers of vehicles involved

879 At an incident someone is unconscious. Your THREE main priorities should be to

Mark three answers
- [ ] A. sweep up the broken glass
- [ ] B. take the names of witnesses
- [ ] C. count the number of vehicles involved
- [ ] D. check the airway is clear
- [ ] E. make sure they are breathing
- [ ] F. stop any heavy bleeding

880 You have stopped at an incident to give help. Which THREE things should you do?

Mark three answers
- [ ] A. Keep injured people warm and comfortable
- [ ] B. Keep injured people calm by talking to them reassuringly
- [ ] C. Keep injured people on the move by walking them around
- [ ] D. Give injured people a warm drink
- [ ] E. Make sure that injured people are not left alone

881 You arrive at an incident. It has just happened and someone is injured. Which THREE should be given urgent priority?

Mark three answers
- [ ] A. Stop any severe bleeding
- [ ] B. Give them a warm drink
- [ ] C. Check they are breathing
- [ ] D. Take numbers of vehicles involved
- [ ] E. Look for witnesses
- [ ] F. Clear their airway and keep it open

882 At an incident a casualty has stopped breathing. You should

Mark two answers
- [ ] A. remove anything that is blocking the mouth
- [ ] B. keep the head tilted forwards as far as possible
- [ ] C. raise the legs to help with circulation
- [ ] D. try to give the casualty something to drink
- [ ] E. tilt the head back gently to clear the airway

883 You are at the scene of an incident. Someone is suffering from shock. You should

Mark four answers
- [ ] A. reassure them constantly
- [ ] B. offer them a cigarette
- [ ] C. keep them warm
- [ ] D. avoid moving them if possible
- [ ] E. avoid leaving them alone
- [ ] F. give them a warm drink

884 Which of the following should you NOT do at the scene of a collision?

Mark one answer
- [ ] A. Warn other traffic by switching on your hazard warning lights
- [ ] B. Call the emergency services immediately
- [ ] C. Offer someone a cigarette to calm them down
- [ ] D. Ask drivers to switch off their engines

885 There has been a collision. A driver is suffering from shock. What TWO of these should you do?

Mark two answers
- [ ] **A.** Give them a drink
- [ ] **B.** Reassure them
- [ ] **C.** Not leave them alone
- [ ] **D.** Offer them a cigarette
- [ ] **E.** Ask who caused the incident

886 You have to treat someone for shock at the scene of an incident. You should

Mark one answer
- [ ] **A.** reassure them constantly
- [ ] **B.** walk them around to calm them down
- [ ] **C.** give them something cold to drink
- [ ] **D.** cool them down as soon as possible

887 You arrive at the scene of a motorcycle crash. No other vehicle is involved. The rider is unconscious and lying in the middle of the road. The FIRST thing you should do is

Mark one answer
- [ ] **A.** move the rider out of the road
- [ ] **B.** warn other traffic
- [ ] **C.** clear the road of debris
- [ ] **D.** give the rider reassurance

888 At an incident a small child is not breathing. To restore normal breathing you should breathe into their mouth

Mark one answer
- [ ] **A.** sharply
- [ ] **B.** gently
- [ ] **C.** heavily
- [ ] **D.** rapidly

889 At an incident a casualty is not breathing. To start the process to restore normal breathing you should

Mark three answers
- [ ] **A.** tilt their head forward
- [ ] **B.** clear the airway
- [ ] **C.** turn them on their side
- [ ] **D.** tilt their head back gently
- [ ] **E.** pinch the nostrils together
- [ ] **F.** put their arms across their chest

890 You arrive at the scene of an incident. There has been an engine fire and someone's hands and arms have been burnt. You should NOT

Mark one answer
- [ ] **A.** douse the burn thoroughly with clean cool non-toxic liquid
- [ ] **B.** lay the casualty down on the ground
- [ ] **C.** remove anything sticking to the burn
- [ ] **D.** reassure them confidently and repeatedly

891 You arrive at an incident where someone is suffering from severe burns. You should

Mark one answer
- [ ] **A.** apply lotions to the injury
- [ ] **B.** burst any blisters
- [ ] **C.** remove anything stuck to the burns
- [ ] **D.** douse the burns with clean cool non-toxic liquid

892 You arrive at an incident. A pedestrian has a severe bleeding leg wound. It is not broken and there is nothing in the wound. What TWO of these should you do?

Mark two answers

- A. Dab the wound to stop bleeding
- B. Keep both legs flat on the ground
- C. Apply firm pressure to the wound
- D. Raise the leg to lessen bleeding
- E. Fetch them a warm drink

893 You arrive at the scene of a crash. Someone is bleeding badly from an arm wound. There is nothing embedded in it. What should you do?

Mark one answer

- A. Apply pressure over the wound and keep the arm down
- B. Dab the wound
- C. Get them a drink
- D. Apply pressure over the wound and raise the arm

894 At an incident a casualty is unconscious but still breathing. You should only move them if

Mark one answer

- A. an ambulance is on its way
- B. bystanders advise you to
- C. there is further danger
- D. bystanders will help you to

895 At a collision you suspect a casualty has back injuries. The area is safe. You should

Mark one answer

- A. offer them a drink
- B. not move them
- C. raise their legs
- D. not call an ambulance

896 At an incident it is important to look after the casualty. When the area is safe, you should

Mark one answer

- A. get them out of the vehicle
- B. give them a drink
- C. give them something to eat
- D. keep them in the vehicle

897 A tanker is involved in a collision. Which sign shows that it is carrying dangerous goods?

Mark one answer

- A. LONG VEHICLE
- B. 2YE 1089
- C.
- D.

898 You are involved in a collision. Because of this which THREE of these documents may the police ask you to produce?

Mark three answers

- A. Vehicle registration document
- B. Driving licence
- C. Theory test certificate
- D. Insurance certificate
- E. MOT test certificate
- F. Vehicle service record

899 You see a car on the hard shoulder of a motorway with a HELP pennant displayed. This means the driver is most likely to be

Mark one answer

- A. a disabled person
- B. first aid trained
- C. a foreign visitor
- D. a rescue patrol person

900 On the motorway, the hard shoulder should be used

Mark one answer

A. to answer a mobile phone
B. when an emergency arises
C. for a short rest when tired
D. to check a road atlas

901 For which TWO should you use hazard warning lights?

Mark two answers

A. When you slow down quickly on a motorway because of a hazard ahead
B. When you have broken down
C. When you wish to stop on double yellow lines
D. When you need to park on the pavement

902 When are you allowed to use hazard warning lights?

Mark one answer

A. When stopped and temporarily obstructing traffic
B. When travelling during darkness without headlights
C. When parked for shopping on double yellow lines
D. When travelling slowly because you are lost

903 You are on a motorway. A large box falls onto the road from a lorry. The lorry does not stop. You should

Mark one answer

A. go to the next emergency telephone and inform the police
B. catch up with the lorry and try to get the driver's attention
C. stop close to the box until the police arrive
D. pull over to the hard shoulder, then remove the box

904 There has been a collision. A motorcyclist is lying injured and unconscious. Unless it is essential, why should you usually NOT attempt to remove their helmet?

Mark one answer

A. Because they may not want you to
B. This could result in more serious injury
C. They will get too cold if you do this
D. Because you could scratch the helmet

905 After a collision, someone is unconscious in their vehicle. When should you call the emergency services?

Mark one answer

A. Only as a last resort
B. As soon as possible
C. After you have woken them up
D. After checking for broken bones

906 A casualty has an injured arm. They can move it freely, but it is bleeding. Why should you get them to keep it in a raised position?

Mark one answer

A. Because it will ease the pain
B. It will help them to be seen more easily
C. To stop them touching other people
D. It will help to reduce the blood flow

907 You are going through a congested tunnel and have to stop. What should you do?

Mark one answer

A. Pull up very close to the vehicle in front to save space
B. Ignore any message signs as they are never up to date
C. Keep a safe distance from the vehicle in front
D. Make a U-turn and find another route

908 You are going through a long tunnel. What will warn you of congestion or an incident ahead?

Mark one answer

- A. Hazard warning lines
- B. Other drivers flashing their lights
- C. Variable message signs
- D. Areas marked with hatch markings

909 You are going through a tunnel. What systems are provided to warn of any incidents, collisions or congestion?

Mark one answer

- A. Double white centre lines
- B. Variable message signs
- C. Chevron 'distance markers'
- D. Rumble strips

910 While driving, a warning light on your vehicle's instrument panel comes on. You should

Mark one answer

- A. continue if the engine sounds alright
- B. hope that it is just a temporary electrical fault
- C. deal with the problem when there is more time
- D. check out the problem quickly and safely

911 You have broken down on a two-way road. You have a warning triangle. You should place the warning triangle at least how far from your vehicle?

Mark one answer

- A. 5 metres (16 feet)
- B. 25 metres (82 feet)
- C. 45 metres (147 feet)
- D. 100 metres (328 feet)

912 You break down on a level crossing. The lights have not yet begun to flash. Which THREE things should you do?

Mark three answers

- A. Telephone the signal operator
- B. Leave your vehicle and get everyone clear
- C. Walk down the track and signal the next train
- D. Move the vehicle if a signal operator tells you to
- E. Tell drivers behind what has happened

913 Your vehicle has broken down on an automatic railway level crossing. What should you do FIRST?

Mark one answer

- A. Get everyone out of the vehicle and clear of the crossing
- B. Telephone your vehicle recovery service to move it
- C. Walk along the track to give warning to any approaching trains
- D. Try to push the vehicle clear of the crossing as soon as possible

914 Your tyre bursts while you are driving. Which TWO things should you do?

Mark two answers

- A. Pull on the handbrake
- B. Brake as quickly as possible
- C. Pull up slowly at the side of the road
- D. Hold the steering wheel firmly to keep control
- E. Continue on at a normal speed

915 Which TWO things should you do when a front tyre bursts?

Mark two answers

- A. Apply the handbrake to stop the vehicle
- B. Brake firmly and quickly
- C. Let the vehicle roll to a stop
- D. Hold the steering wheel lightly
- E. Grip the steering wheel firmly

916 Your vehicle has a puncture on a motorway. What should you do?

Mark one answer
- **A.** Drive slowly to the next service area to get assistance
- **B.** Pull up on the hard shoulder. Change the wheel as quickly as possible
- **C.** Pull up on the hard shoulder. Use the emergency phone to get assistance
- **D.** Switch on your hazard lights. Stop in your lane

917 Which THREE of these items should you carry for use in the event of a collision?

Mark three answers
- **A.** Road map
- **B.** Can of petrol
- **C.** Jump leads
- **D.** Fire extinguisher
- **E.** First aid kit
- **F.** Warning triangle

918 You are in a collision on a two-way road. You have a warning triangle with you. At what distance before the obstruction should you place the warning triangle?

Mark one answer
- **A.** 25 metres (82 feet)
- **B.** 45 metres (147 feet)
- **C.** 100 metres (328 feet)
- **D.** 150 metres (492 feet)

919 You have broken down on a two-way road. You have a warning triangle. It should be displayed

Mark one answer
- **A.** on the roof of your vehicle
- **B.** at least 150 metres (492 feet) behind your vehicle
- **C.** at least 45 metres (147 feet) behind your vehicle
- **D.** just behind your vehicle

920 You have stalled in the middle of a level crossing and cannot restart the engine. The warning bell starts to ring. You should

Mark one answer
- **A.** get out and clear of the crossing
- **B.** run down the track to warn the signal operator
- **C.** carry on trying to restart the engine
- **D.** push the vehicle clear of the crossing

921 You are on the motorway. Luggage falls from your vehicle. What should you do?

Mark one answer
- **A.** Stop at the next emergency telephone and contact the police
- **B.** Stop on the motorway and put on hazard lights while you pick it up
- **C.** Walk back up the motorway to pick it up
- **D.** Pull up on the hard shoulder and wave traffic down

922 You are on a motorway. When can you use hazard warning lights?

Mark two answers
- **A.** When a vehicle is following too closely
- **B.** When you slow down quickly because of danger ahead
- **C.** When you are towing another vehicle
- **D.** When driving on the hard shoulder
- **E.** When you have broken down on the hard shoulder

923

You are in collision with another moving vehicle. Someone is injured and your vehicle is damaged. Which FOUR of the following should you find out?

Mark four answers

A. Whether the driver owns the other vehicle involved

B. The other driver's name, address and telephone number

C. The make and registration number of the other vehicle

D. The occupation of the other driver

E. The details of the other driver's vehicle insurance

F. Whether the other driver is licensed to drive

924

You have broken down on a motorway. When you use the emergency telephone you will be asked

Mark three answers

A. for the number on the telephone that you are using

B. for your driving licence details

C. for the name of your vehicle insurance company

D. for details of yourself and your vehicle

E. whether you belong to a motoring organisation

925

You lose control of your car and damage a garden wall. No one is around. What must you do?

Mark one answer   **NI**

A. Report the incident to the police within 24 hours

B. Go back to tell the house owner the next day

C. Report the incident to your insurance company when you get home

D. Find someone in the area to tell them about it immediately

926

Your engine catches fire. What should you do first?

Mark one answer

A. Lift the bonnet and disconnect the battery

B. Lift the bonnet and warn other traffic

C. Call a breakdown service

D. Call the fire brigade

927

Before driving through a tunnel what should you do?

Mark one answer

A. Switch your radio off

B. Remove any sunglasses

C. Close your sunroof

D. Switch on windscreen wipers

928

You are driving through a tunnel and the traffic is flowing normally. What should you do?

Mark one answer

A. Use parking lights

B. Use front spot lights

C. Use dipped headlights

D. Use rear fog lights

929

When approaching a tunnel it is good advice to

Mark one answer

A. put on your sunglasses and use the sun visor

B. check your tyre pressures

C. change down to a lower gear

D. make sure your radio is tuned to the frequency shown

930

You are driving through a tunnel. Your vehicle breaks down. What should you do?

Mark one answer

A. Switch on hazard warning lights

B. Remain in your vehicle

C. Wait for the police to find you

D. Rely on CCTV cameras seeing you

931 Your vehicle breaks down in a tunnel. What should you do?

Mark one answer

- A. Stay in your vehicle and wait for the police
- B. Stand in the lane behind your vehicle to warn others
- C. Stand in front of your vehicle to warn oncoming drivers
- D. Switch on hazard lights then go and call for help immediately

932 You have a collision while driving through a tunnel. You are not injured but your vehicle cannot be driven. What should you do FIRST?

Mark one answer

- A. Rely on other drivers phoning for the police
- B. Switch off the engine and switch on hazard lights
- C. Take the names of witnesses and other drivers
- D. Sweep up any debris that is in the road

933 When driving through a tunnel you should

Mark one answer

- A. Look out for variable message signs
- B. Use your air conditioning system
- C. Switch on your rear fog lights
- D. Always use your windscreen wipers

934 What TWO safeguards could you take against fire risk to your vehicle?

Mark two answers

- A. Keep water levels above maximum
- B. Carry a fire extinguisher
- C. Avoid driving with a full tank of petrol
- D. Use unleaded petrol
- E. Check out any strong smell of petrol
- F. Use low octane fuel

935 Your vehicle catches fire while driving through a tunnel. It is still driveable. What should you do?

Mark one answer

- A. Leave it where it is with the engine running
- B. Pull up, then walk to an emergency telephone point
- C. Park it away from the carriageway
- D. Drive it out of the tunnel if you can do so

936 You are driving through a tunnel. Your vehicle catches fire. What should you do?

Mark one answer

- A. Continue through the tunnel if you can
- B. Turn your vehicle around immediately
- C. Reverse out of the tunnel
- D. Carry out an emergency stop

937 You are in a tunnel. Your vehicle is on fire and you CANNOT drive it. What should you do?

Mark two answers

- A. Stay in the vehicle and close the windows
- B. Switch on hazard warning lights
- C. Leave the engine running
- D. Try and put out the fire
- E. Switch off all of your lights
- F. Wait for other people to phone for help

938 You are driving through a tunnel. There has been a collision and the car in front is on fire and blocking the road. What should you do?

Mark one answer

- A. Overtake and continue as quickly as you can
- B. Lock all the doors and windows
- C. Switch on hazard warning lights
- D. Stop, then reverse out of the tunnel

939 You are at an incident where a casualty is unconscious. Their breathing should be checked. This should be done for at least

Mark one answer
- [ ] A. 2 seconds
- [ ] B. 10 seconds
- [ ] C. 1 minute
- [ ] D. 2 minutes

940 Following a collision someone has suffered a burn. The burn needs to be cooled. What is the shortest time it should be cooled for?

Mark one answer
- [ ] A. 5 minutes
- [ ] B. 10 minutes
- [ ] C. 15 minutes
- [ ] D. 20 minutes

941 After a collision someone has suffered a burn. The burn needs to be cooled. What is the shortest time it should be cooled for?

Mark one answer
- [ ] A. 30 seconds
- [ ] B. 60 seconds
- [ ] C. 5 minutes
- [ ] D. 10 minutes

942 A casualty is not breathing normally. Chest compressions should be given. At what rate?

Mark one answer
- [ ] A. 50 per minute
- [ ] B. 100 per minute
- [ ] C. 200 per minute
- [ ] D. 250 per minute

943 An adult casualty is not breathing. To maintain circulation, compressions should be given. What is the correct depth to press?

Mark one answer
- [ ] A. 1 to 2 centimetres
- [ ] B. 4 to 5 centimetres
- [ ] C. 10 to 15 centimetres
- [ ] D. 15 to 20 centimetres

944 A person has been injured. They may be suffering from shock. What are the warning signs to look for?

Mark one answer
- [ ] A. Flushed complexion
- [ ] B. Warm dry skin
- [ ] C. Slow pulse
- [ ] D. Pale grey skin

945 You suspect that an injured person may be suffering from shock. What are the warning signs to look for?

Mark one answer
- [ ] A. Warm dry skin
- [ ] B. Sweating
- [ ] C. Slow pulse
- [ ] D. Skin rash

946 An injured person has been placed in the recovery position. They are unconscious but breathing normally. What else should be done?

Mark one answer
- [ ] A. Press firmly between the shoulders
- [ ] B. Place their arms by their side
- [ ] C. Give them a hot sweet drink
- [ ] D. Check the airway is clear

947 An injured motorcyclist is lying unconscious in the road. You should always

Mark one answer
- [ ] A. remove the safey helmet
- [ ] B. seek medical assistance
- [ ] C. move the person off the road
- [ ] D. remove the leather jacket

948 You have a collision whilst your car is moving. What is the FIRST thing you must do?

Mark one answer
- [ ] A. Stop only if someone waves at you
- [ ] B. Call the emergency services
- [ ] C. Stop at the scene of the incident
- [ ] D. Call your insurance company

949
You are towing a small trailer on a busy three-lane motorway. All the lanes are open. You must

Mark two answers
- A. not exceed 60mph
- B. not overtake
- C. have a stabiliser fitted
- D. use only the left and centre lanes

950
Any load that is carried on a roof rack should be

Mark one answer
- A. securely fastened when driving
- B. loaded towards the rear of the vehicle
- C. visible in your exterior mirror
- D. covered with plastic sheeting

951
You are planning to tow a caravan. Which of these will mostly help to aid the vehicle handling?

Mark one answer
- A. A jockey wheel fitted to the tow bar
- B. Power steering fitted to the towing vehicle
- C. Anti-lock brakes fitted to the towing vehicle
- D. A stabiliser fitted to the tow bar

952
If a trailer swerves or snakes when you are towing it you should

Mark one answer
- A. ease off the accelerator and reduce your speed
- B. let go of the steering wheel and let it correct itself
- C. brake hard and hold the pedal down
- D. increase your speed as quickly as possible

953
How can you stop a caravan snaking from side to side?

Mark one answer
- A. Turn the steering wheel slowly to each side
- B. Accelerate to increase your speed
- C. Stop as quickly as you can
- D. Slow down very gradually

954
On which TWO occasions might you inflate your tyres to more than the recommended normal pressure?

Mark two answers
- A. When the roads are slippery
- B. When driving fast for a long distance
- C. When the tyre tread is worn below 2mm
- D. When carrying a heavy load
- E. When the weather is cold
- F. When the vehicle is fitted with anti-lock brakes

955
A heavy load on your roof rack will

Mark one answer
- A. improve the road holding
- B. reduce the stopping distance
- C. make the steering lighter
- D. reduce stability

956
Are passengers allowed to ride in a caravan that is being towed?

Mark one answer
- A. Yes, if they are over 14
- B. No, not at any time
- C. Only if all the seats in the towing vehicle are full
- D. Only if a stabiliser is fitted

957 You are towing a caravan along a motorway. The caravan begins to swerve from side to side. What should you do?

Mark one answer

- [ ] **A.** Ease off the accelerator slowly
- [ ] **B.** Steer sharply from side to side
- [ ] **C.** Do an emergency stop
- [ ] **D.** Speed up very quickly

958 A trailer must stay securely hitched up to the towing vehicle. What additional safety device can be fitted to the trailer braking system?

Mark one answer

- [ ] **A.** Stabiliser
- [ ] **B.** Jockey wheel
- [ ] **C.** Corner steadies
- [ ] **D.** Breakaway cable

959 Overloading your vehicle can seriously affect the

Mark two answers

- [ ] **A.** gearbox
- [ ] **B.** steering
- [ ] **C.** handling
- [ ] **D.** battery life
- [ ] **E.** journey time

960 Who is responsible for making sure that a vehicle is not overloaded?

Mark one answer

- [ ] **A.** The driver of the vehicle
- [ ] **B.** The owner of the items being carried
- [ ] **C.** The person who loaded the vehicle
- [ ] **D.** The licensing authority

961 You are carrying a child in your car. They are under three years of age. Which of these is a suitable restraint?

Mark one answer

- [ ] **A.** A child seat
- [ ] **B.** An adult holding a child
- [ ] **C.** An adult seat belt
- [ ] **D.** An adult lap belt

962 Why would you fit a stabiliser before towing a caravan?

Mark one answer

- [ ] **A.** It will help with stability when driving in crosswinds
- [ ] **B.** It will allow heavy items to be loaded behind the axle
- [ ] **C.** It will help you to raise and lower the jockey wheel
- [ ] **D.** It will allow you to tow without the breakaway cable

963 You wish to tow a trailer. Where would you find the maximum noseweight of your vehicle's tow ball?

Mark one answer

- [ ] **A.** In the vehicle handbook
- [ ] **B.** In The Highway Code
- [ ] **C.** In your vehicle registration certificate
- [ ] **D.** In your licence documents

ALERTNESS – SECTION 1

1 C	2 BDF	3 C	4 D	5 C	6 C	7 C	8 C	9 B
10 D	11 AC	12 ABCD	13 AD	14 AB	15 AB	16 ABCD	17 B	18 D
19 B	20 D	21 B	22 B	23 ABE	24 C	25 B	26 B	27 D
28 C	29 C	30 C	31 A	32 D	33 D	34 B	35 A	36 D
37 B								

ATTITUDE – SECTION 2

38 D	39 A	40 C	41 B	42 C	43 D	44 D	45 B	46 B
47 BCD	48 ABE	49 A	50 D	51 B	52 A	53 A	54 B	55 A
56 A	57 C	58 A	59 B	60 D	61 D	62 D	63 A	64 A
65 B	66 C	67 A	68 C	69 A	70 C	71 B	72 C	73 DE
74 B	75 D	76 B	77 C	78 AB	79 D	80 C	81 A	82 A
83 B	84 A	85 D	86 C	87 C				

SAFETY AND YOUR VEHICLE – SECTION 3

88 B	89 AB	90 ABF	91 BEF	92 C	93 ACF	94 C	95 B	96 D
97 C	98 D	99 D	100 D	101 A	102 AE	103 D	104 B	105 D
106 D	107 A	108 B	109 D	110 D	111 BC	112 BC	113 A	114 D
115 A	116 B	117 B	118 D	119 C	120 D	121 D	122 D	123 B
124 B	125 B	126 D	127 ABF	128 ABC	129 ABC	130 BDF	131 ADE	132 BD
133 B	134 CDE	135 B	136 B	137 C	138 B	139 DE	140 A	141 C
142 B	143 D	144 D	145 D	146 B	147 C	148 A	149 B	150 D
151 C	152 A	153 B	154 AB	155 A	156 D	157 B	158 BCD	159 C
160 CD	161 A	162 A	163 D	164 C	165 B	166 B	167 B	168 D
169 ABE	170 ADE	171 D	172 A	173 B	174 C	175 D	176 A	177B
178 C	179 D	180 A	181 C	182 D	183 B	184 A	185 B	186 D
187 B	188 A	189 C	190 D	191 B	192 B	193 D	194 B	195 B
196 C	197 A	198 A	199 A					

SAFETY MARGINS – SECTION 4

200 D	201 D	202 BC	203 B	204 D	205 D	206 C	207 C	208 A
209 B	210 A	211 B	212 A	213 B	214 AE	215 C	216 C	217 BDEF
218 B	219 D	220 A	221 C	222 A	223 AD	224 C	225 B	226 B
227 B	228 C	229 C	230 B	231 B	232 BC	233 C	234 C	235 B
236 C	237 D	238 BC	239 B	240 ACE	241 D	242 D	243 D	244 A
245 D	246 BD	247 D	248 B	249 A	250 D	251 C	252 B	253 B
254 C	255 A	256 A	257 D	258 ACD				

Answers to Questions

HAZARD AWARENESS – SECTION 5

259 D	260 CD	261 B	262 C	263 A	264 D	265 ACE	266 D	267 C
268 C	269 C	270 D	271 B	272 B	273 A	274 A	275 A	276 C
277 C	278 CD	279 A	280 B	281 A	282 C	283 BF	284 B	285 AE
286 A	287 D	288 D	289 C	290 B	291 B	292 C	293 A	294 B
295 B	296 CD	297 B	298 D	299 B	300 A	301 A	302 D	303 A
304 B	305 AE	306 C	307 B	308 BC	309 D	310 B	311 B	312 C
313 D	314 C	315 CD	316 AC	317 AB	318 A	319 A	320 B	321 B
322 ABC	323 C	324 C	325 C	326 ABE	327 C	328 D	329 D	330 C
331 C	332 D	333 ABD	334 ABC	335 D	336 C	337 AB	338 B	339 B
340 CD	341 D	342 ACE	343 ABE	344 A	345 A	346 D	347 D	348 A
349 D	350 A	351 A	352 B	353 B	354 ACE			

VULNERABLE ROAD USERS – SECTION 6

355 D	356 D	357 C	358 C	359 B	360 D	361 D	362 D	363 B
364 C	365 D	366 A	367 D	368 D	369 B	370 D	371 B	372 D
373 D	374 C	375 AC	376 C	377 C	378 A	379 D	380 C	381 D
382 ABC	383 C	384 B	385 AC	386 ABD	387 B	388 D	389 A	390 A
391 D	392 D	393 A	394 A	395 C	396 C	397 C	398 D	399 D
400 B	401 A	402 C	403 D	404 C	405 C	406 A	407 D	408 D
409 A	410 A	411 B	412 B	413 D	414 C	415 C	416 B	417 C
418 AE	419 D	420 C	421 C	422 B	423 B	424 D	425 A	426 C
427 D	428 D	429 B	430 D	431 B	432 B	433 C	434 D	435 A

OTHER TYPES OF VEHICLE – SECTION 7

436 A	437 A	438 B	439 B	440 D	441 B	442 A	443 BC	444 B
445 D	446 A	447 A	448 C	449 B	450 D	451 D	452 D	453 B
454 B	455 B	456 AC	457 BD	458 B	459 D	460 D	461 A	462 A

VEHICLE HANDLING – SECTION 8

463 ACE	464 A	465 CD	466 D	467 A	468 BDF	469 C	470 D	471 C
472 DE	473 B	474 C	475 C	476 D	477 D	478 C	479 C	480 BD
481 BD	482 D	483 B	484 C	485 CE	486 C	487 D	488 A	489 A
490 C	491 B	492 ABDF	493 A	494 D	495 B	496 B	497 AB	498 BD
499 A	500 ACD	501 B	502 A	503 C	504 B	505 A	506 A	507 C
508 C	509 A	510 B	511 C	512 D	513 B	514 D	515 ABD	516 D
517 C	518 C	519 C	520 D	521 D	522 A	523 B	524 B	

Answers to Questions

MOTORWAY RULES – SECTION 9

525 ADEF	526 ADEF	527 D	528 D	529 D	530 D	531 A	532 B	533 C
534 D	535 C	536 A	537 C	538 A	539 D	540 A	541 C	542 C
543 C	544 C	545 C	546 C	547 B	548 C	549 B	550 B	551 A
552 B	553 B	554 D	555 CDF	556 C	557 D	558 C	559 D	560 A
561 B	562 B	563 D	564 C	565 A	566 B	567 D	568 A	569 D
570 D	571 A	572 C	573 B	574 B	575 C	576 A	577 A	578 B
579 D	580 D	581 B	582 D	583 D	584 B	585 C	586 D	587 D
588 C	589 A	590 D	591 B					

RULES OF THE ROAD – SECTION 10

592 C	593 C	594 D	595 B	596 A	597 C	598 D	599 ADF	600 AD
601 A	602 B	603 A	604 B	605 A	606 D	607 A	608 D	609 D
610 C	611 A	612 ACE	613 B	614 C	615 D	616 BD	617 B	618 A
619 D	620 C	621 A	622 B	623 CDE	624 B	625 AE	626 B	627 A
628 ABD	629 A	630 B	631 B	632 A	633 D	634 A	635 D	636 C
637 D	638 D	639 D	640 D	641 D	642 C	643 C	644 D	645 A
646 A	647 A	648 C	649 B	650 A	651 D	652 AB	653 A	654 D
655 D	656 A	657 D	658 B	659 ABC	660 D	661 A	662 D	663 A
664 A	665 B	666 C						

ROAD AND TRAFFIC SIGNS – SECTION 11

667 D	668 D	669 A	670 A	671 B	672 A	673 D	674 B	675 D
676 D	677 D	678 A	679 C	680 B	681 D	682 C	683 B	684 A
685 B	686 B	687 C	688 C	689 A	690 C	691 B	692 C	693 B
694 D	695 D	696 C	697 D	698 C	699 B	700 C	701 D	702 A
703 D	704 B	705 D	706 B	707 A	708 A	709 A	710 A	711 B
712 B	713 A	714 D	715 ACEF	716 C	717 A	718 A	719 C	720 D
721 B	722 C	723 B	724 B	725 B	726 B	727 D	728 A	729 C
730 A	731 C	732 D	733 A	734 C	735 B	736 D	737 A	738 B
739 B	740 C	741 C	742 A	743 A	744 C	745 C	746 B	747 D
748 C	749 B	750 A	751 C	752 D	753 C	754 B	755 A	756 A
757 C	758 BDF	759 A	760 C	761 C	762 B	763 B	764 A	765 C
766 A	767 B	768 A	769 B	770 D	771 B	772 A	773 D	774 C
775 D	776 C	777 B	778 C	779 C	780 A	781 B	782 D	783 B
784 B	785 A	786 D	787 A	788 B	789 B	790 D	791 C	792 B
793 A	794 B	795 B	796 C	797 A	798 B	799 A	800 A	801 C
802 C	803 A	804 B	805 C	806 B	807 A	808 C	809 A	810 A
811 C	812 C	813 B	814 B	815 B	816 A	817 B	818 B	819 A
820 D	821 B	822 D						

Answers to Questions

DOCUMENTS – SECTION 12

823 C	824 B	825 B	826 BE	827 C	828 C	829 B	830 D	831 AB
832 D	833 D	834 CDE	835 C	836 B	837 B	838 C	839 ABF	840 BCE
841 ABE	842 BD	843 D	844 A	845 C	846 ABD	847 D	848 B	849 C
850 A	851 C	852 C	853 D	854 B	855 C	856 D	857 B	858 A
859 B	860 D	861 A	862 AB	863 A	864 D	865 D	866 ABD	867 A
868 C	869 C							

ACCIDENTS – SECTION 13

870 A	871 BD	872 B	873 ABE	874 A	875 ACF	876 A	877 ABD	878 ACE
879 DEF	880 ABE	881 ACF	882 AE	883 ACDE	884 C	885 BC	886 A	887 B
888 B	889 BDE	890 C	891 D	892 CD	893 D	894 C	895 B	896 D
897 B	898 BDE	899 A	900 B	901 AB	902 A	903 A	904 B	905 B
906 D	907 C	908 C	909 B	910 D	911 C	912 ABD	913 A	914 CD
915 CE	916 C	917 DEF	918 B	919 C	920 A	921 A	922 BE	923 ABCE
924 ADE	925 A	926 D	927 B	928 C	929 D	930 A	931 D	932 B
933 A	934 BE	935 D	936 A	937 BD	938 C	939 B	940 B	941 D
942 B	943 B	944 D	945 B	946 D	947 B	948 C		

VEHICLE LOADING – SECTION 14

949 AD	950 A	951 D	952 A	953 D	954 BD	955 D	956 B	957 A
958 D	959 BC	960 A	961 A	962 A	963 A			